Network Now

English

A1

Teacher's Resource Book

Lynda Hübner

Langenscheidt

Berlin · Madrid · München · Warschau · Wien · Zürich

Contents

Welcome to the *Teacher's Resource Book* for *Network Now A1*

Your course: *Network Now A1*

- *Network Now A1* provides 24 ninety-minute lessons, covering a one year (2 semester) course.
- Each of the 6 units has 3 steps (18 lessons), followed by a revision lesson, *Now I can* (6 lessons).
- If your course has more than 24 lessons and you need **extra lessons**,
  - use the ***Zero lesson*** on pages 5–7 of this book for your first course contact.
  - use the ***Globetrotter*** pages. There are two *Globetrotter* pages – a *Globetrotter Work* and a *Globetrotter Travel* page after Units 2, 4 and 6, and you can find ideas on how to use them in class in this *Resource Book* (pages 122 ff.). Each of these pages provides forty-five minutes of classroom material and a further forty-five minutes of activities are available on the Internet.
  - use the ***Christmas lesson*** on pages 127 ff. of this book.

Your *Network Now A1* lessons

- Each step of the 3-step unit is designed to last for 90 minutes. In each step there is a reading input, a listening input, grammar, vocabulary and functional English.
- The fourth lesson in the unit, *Now I can*, is a review lesson and it mirrors the list of learning aims on the introductory page of each unit – the *Photo page*.
- If your lessons are longer than 90 minutes, or if you want to have **something extra for your lesson**, you can find materials here:
  - In every step, there's a reference to the ***Language and culture*** section – texts and tasks about linguistic and cultural aspects of life in English-speaking countries – and this can be done in class or set for homework as the tasks have keys. Recordings of the texts can be found online.
  - The ***Reading*** pages, which are part of the *Selfstudy* for each Step 3, can also be used in class. Ideas for exploiting the *Reading* texts can be found in this *Resource Book* (pages 119 ff.).
  - This ***Teacher's Resource Book*** provides ideas for more activities in each step (pages 80 ff.), and has a resource section of photocopiable materials and templates (pages 98 ff.).
  - Download the extra *A1* materials from the Internet – see **www.langenscheidt.de/networknow/activities**
  - Download extra materials from the *Network Teachers' Club* – see **www.langenscheidt.de/network/club**

Your *Teacher's Resource Book* for *Network Now A1*

The ***Teacher's Resource Book*** (TRB) is divided into **three main parts:**

Part 1: Lesson notes

- The lesson notes give detailed **instructions** on how to organise activities and teach the structures.
- Approximate **timings** are given for each activity – and what to do if you're short of time.
- There are **keys** to the activities on the classroom pages, where appropriate.
- If an activity involves a listening exercise, you'll find the **audio script** framed on the page and the **track numbers** are given with the relevant activities: 2/13 = CD number 2, track 13. The ▶ indicates when the track is to be played.
- Some of the information in the notes is printed in grey – this means it's an optional activity.
- Suggestions are made on how to make some exercises simpler (↓) or more complex (↑).
- Some activities offer the students a choice of complexity. The one-star* option is slightly easier than the standard, two-star** option and the three-star*** option is more challenging. Each student can decide for him- / herself the degree to which he / she wants to be challenged.
- And look out for these useful elements:
  Tip – a teaching tip which can be used at this particular stage of the lesson (see page 8).
  ! – a reminder about some aspect of what you're about to teach (see page 9).
  NB – a relevant piece of information for this step (see page 11).

→

Part 2: Optional & additional materials – Getting ready for Unit (1)

This section provides extra activities for each step and each *Now I can*. It should be looked at before the lesson as some of the activities require preparation.

- **FYI (For Your Information):** This guides you to topic-related information on the Internet. It isn't intended for the students, but as background information for the teacher.
- **Preparing Unit (1), (Step 1):**
  – Extra activities for the step or for *Now I can*.
  – Notes on dealing with the *Language and culture* texts and tasks in class.
  – A link to the downloadable activity for this step or for *Now I can*.

Part 3: Optional & additional materials – Photocopiable activities

- There are **photocopiable materials** to accompany the extra activities for the **steps** in Part 2.
- And there's also a **template** to accompany the extra activities for the ***Now I can*** of each unit. These templates can be filled in and used in a variety of ways at different levels – so you can have a 'tailor-made' activity for your class.

So all it remains for the *Network* team to say is: Enjoy your teaching with *Network Now A1*.

The Zero lesson

In the first lesson, not all students have the coursebook, so here are some ideas for classroom activities which you can do without your students needing a coursebook. The aim is to encourage students to get to know each other and get used to working together. The activities are also confidence-builders and help learners to overcome their inhibitions in speaking.

In this first lesson, there will, inevitably, be some German spoken. The golden rule about German in the lesson is: *As little as possible but as much as necessary.*

For some of the activities on this page, each student will need a copy of the **worksheet** (page 6).
And if you want to find out more about your students, their linguistic backgrounds and their expectations, ask them to fill in the **Learner profile**. For this, each student will need a copy of page 7.

1 **Introductions:** Introduce yourself to the class: *Hello, my name's (Eva). Nice to see you again, (Bernd). / Nice to meet you.*
Some students may be surprised at the use of first names and will need reassuring that it's common practice in English-speaking countries.
If there are several students in the group who know each other, get them to introduce each other to the new students, giving the person's name and saying something they know about the person. New students then introduce themselves and volunteer one piece of information.
Students make a name card by folding a piece of paper in half and writing their first name on the front and back of the paper (so that classmates in front of them and next to them can see it).

2 **Getting to know you:** Hand out a copy of the worksheet to each student. Refer them to ▸ **worksheet activity A** and give them time to read it through. Demonstrate the activity by completing some of the relevant sentences about you and inviting students to ask you questions.
First students complete the sentences in writing. Then they sit together in small groups and ask and answer questions about what they have written.
Monitor the activity, joining in when appropriate. Don't worry about correcting mistakes – it's more important in this first lesson that the students get an opportunity to speak and feel comfortable working with people in their class – and that you get a bit of an overview of individual students' abilities. After the activity, they can return to their seats (and their name cards!).

3 **Yes, I do / No, I don't**
This is a milling activity to encourage students to communicate about English, in English. Each student needs a copy of ▸ **worksheet activity B.**

4 **Your coursebook**
Hold up your copy of *Network Now A1*, ask the students to have a copy with them for the next lesson. Give the students time to read about *Now A1* ▸ **worksheet activity C** – and then introduce the characters by reading out the following sentences so that students can complete the information.

Now let me introduce you to the people in Network Now A1. Write in the information. Picture 1: This is Anna. Her family name is Turner – that's T_U_R_N_E_R. Anna Turner. She's from Ottawa. She has a job in Canterbury for a year. Her family was from Faversham originally. Anna goes to a family history class at Faversham college.

Now look at picture 2. Cross out the wrong information. Dave Evans is the teacher of the family history course at Faversham college. He likes history, it's his hobby. And it's his job, too. He's the director of Faversham Museum.

In Picture 3, you can see Susan. Susan Davis. Listen and write in the missing letters. She's in the family history class, too because she's interested in her family history. She's in the same class as Susan. They sit together every week.

Picture 4: Write in the correct words. Susan and Tom are married – Mr and Mrs Davis. He's in the family history class, too. It's one of his hobbies. And his other hobby is cooking; he loves cooking, and eating, Italian food.

5 **Profiles**
Students read the information about Anna ▸ **worksheet activity D.** Then they write their own profile on a piece of paper, replacing the underlined phrases with information about themselves. Collect their papers and ask individual students to read out a profile (they should use the first person: *I* ...). The class guesses whose profile it is.

6 **Learner profile:** Students fill in the Learner profile page (page 7). This is particularly useful to find out about students' previous language experience as there may be students in your class who haven't come directly from a *Network Starter* class. As people finish writing, collect their sheets and chat to individuals about what they've written.

7 **Goodbye:** As the lesson draws to a close, write on the board, as appropriate:

Board: *Goodbye (Tina). See you (next week / tomorrow / on Thursday).*

Get students to say goodbye to you and their neighbours.

The Zero lesson

Worksheet

A **Getting to know you** Vervollständigen Sie die Sätze mit Ihren persönlichen Angaben.

1 My name is ...

2 I live ...

3 I have ...

4 I like ...

5 My favourite ...

6 At the weekend, I ...

7 My last holiday was ...

8 My last English lesson was ...

B **Yes, I do / No, I don't**

Gehen Sie im Klassenraum herum und stellen Sie den anderen Fragen mit *Do you ...?* Wenn Sie als Antwort *Yes, I do.* erhalten, schreiben Sie den Namen der Person auf die Zeile und stellen Sie weitere Fragen. Versuchen Sie, für jede Zeile einen neuen Namen zu finden. Wenn sich alle wieder hingesetzt haben, berichten Sie der Gruppe, was Sie über eine Person im Kurs erfahren haben.

__________________ knows an English-speaking person.

__________________ wants to learn English for work.

__________________ likes speaking English.

__________________ needs English for holidays.

__________________ speaks another language. *(English, German and ...)*

C **Your coursebook: Network Now A1**

Ihr Kursbuch heißt *Network Now A1*. In jeder Lektion lernen Sie alles, um sich in verschiedenen Situationen auf Englisch zurechtzufinden. In jedem *Step* gibt es eine Seite *Language study*. Hier können Sie die Grammatik üben, die Sie im Unterricht gelernt haben. Manchmal gibt es auf dieser Seite zwei Abschnitte: *You already know* (mit der Grammatik, die Sie schon von früher kennen) und *And now* (mit der neuen Grammatik aus der Unterrichtsstunde).

Außerdem gibt es eine Seite *Selfstudy* mit Übungen für zu Hause. Wenn Sie lieber online lernen wollen, finden Sie diese und weitere Übungen auch im Internet unter www.langenscheidt.de/networknow/selfstudy

Und nun lernen Sie einige der Personen kennen, die Sie im Buch treffen werden. Hören Sie Ihrer Kursleiterin / Ihrem Kursleiter zu und vervollständigen Sie die Informationen.

(1)

1 This is Anna ______________. She isn't American, she's ______________.
She has a ______________ in Canterbury.
She goes to a ______________ history class at Faversham college.

(2)

2 Dave Evans is **a student** / **the teacher** at the college. He likes **geography** / **history**. He's the director of **Faversham college** / **Faversham museum**.

(3)

3 Susan Davis is in the
f_ _ _ _ _ h_ _ _ _ _ _
c_ _ _ _, too.
She's in the same class as
S_ _ _ _ and they _ _ _ together.

(4)

4 **boyfriend / cooking / gardening / husband / Italian / Indian**
Tom Davis is Susan's ______________. His hobbies are family history and ______________. He really likes ______________ food.

D **Profiles**

Lesen Sie, was Anna über sich gesagt hat. Schreiben Sie nun Ihr eigenes Profil, indem Sie die unterstrichenen Informationen durch Ihre persönlichen Angaben ersetzen.

I'm from Ontario, in Canada.
My family was from Faversham originally.
I went to school in Ontario.
Now I live in Faversham.
I'm not married and I don't have children.
My hobbies? I like history and sightseeing.
I'm in this class because I want to know more about my family history.

Learner profile

Ihr Lehrer / Ihre Lehrerin möchte gerne mehr über Ihre Erwartungen an diesen Kurs erfahren. Daher wäre es schön, wenn Sie das folgende Profil ausfüllen. Lassen Sie die Fragen, die Sie nicht beantworten möchten, einfach aus.

Name: ____________________

Geburtsort: ____________________

Nationalität: ____________________

Muttersprache(n): ____________________

Wenn Deutsch nicht Ihre Muttersprache ist, welche Aussage trifft auf Ihre Deutschkenntnisse zu:

- ☐ Ich kann vertraute, alltägliche Ausdrücke und ganz einfache Sätze verstehen und verwenden.
- ☐ Ich kann einfache und häufig gebrauchte Ausdrücke verstehen und mich in einfachen routinemäßigen Situationen verständigen.
- ☐ Ich kann die meisten alltäglichen Situationen bewältigen und kann mich einfach und zusammenhängend zu mir vertrauten Themen äußern.
- ☐ Ich kann mich spontan und fließend mit deutschen Muttersprachlern ohne größere Anstrengung auf beiden Seiten verständigen.
- ☐ Ich kann mich spontan und fließend ausdrücken und mich strukturiert und ausführlich zu komplexen Sachverhalten äußern.
- ☐ Ich kann mich sehr spontan, sehr flüssig und ganz genau ausdrücken und auch bei komplexeren Sachverhalten feinere Bedeutungsnuancen deutlich machen.

Welche anderen Sprachen sprechen Sie? ____________________

Haben Sie Englisch in der Schule gelernt? Wenn ja, geben Sie bitte an, an welcher Art Schule, für wie lange und wie lange es her ist.

____

Das hat mir gefallen: ____________________

____

Das hat mir nicht gefallen: ____________________

____

Haben Sie schon einmal einen Englischkurs besucht? Wenn ja, schreiben Sie bitte ein paar Worte dazu:

____

Ich habe aufgehört, weil ____________________

____

Das hat mir gefallen: ____________________

____

Das hat mir nicht gefallen: ____________________

____

Warum möchten Sie Englisch lernen? ____________________

____

Was möchten Sie am Ende des Kurses alles können? ____________________

____

Unit 1 Step 1 Welcome to the class

Contents

Storyline	Anna is from Canada. She's in Faversham for a year and attends a family history class, where she meets Susan and Tom, and the class teacher Dave.
Functions	Introducing people and greeting people; Asking for the meanings of words
Vocabulary	Hobbies and interests
Grammar	**You already know:** *it's* and *they're* **And now:** *this, that, these* and *those*

Lesson notes

Additional material

For optional and additional material for Unit 1, Step 1, see page 80.
Refer to this section before your lesson as some of the materials require preparation.

Optional stages

Optional stages of the lesson are written in grey in these notes.

Tip: Learner profile If you haven't done the *Zero lesson*, copy the *Learner profile* (p. 7) for each student and ask them to fill it in at home. This will help you get to know your students early on in the course.

NB: *Introductions and greetings* were covered in *Exercise 1* of the *Zero lesson*. If you're using Unit 1 Step 1 as the first lesson, do this *Starter* exercise first:

Starter:
Introduce yourself
5– mins

Tip: Name cards Get students to make a name card by folding a piece of paper in half, writing their first name on both sides of the paper (so that the students sitting next to them can also read the name) and standing it on their desk.

Photo page
5– mins

- Say: *Look at page 9* and hold up your open book. Give the students a minute to look at all the pictures. Read the text to the class. Then ask the questions to individual students.
  Anna's from Ottawa, Canada.
- Refer students to *In dieser Unit lernen Sie u. a.: ...* and give them a minute to read the learning aims.

FYI: Ottawa is the capital of Canada. It's in the province of Ontario. Faversham ['fævəʃəm] is a market town 14 km west of Canterbury and 77 km east of London. For more information, read the *Language and culture* texts on page 25 in your coursebook.

Nice to meet you
1/2
5+ mins

- Students listen to the dialogue twice – once with the dialogue covered, and a second time with the dialogue uncovered.

Tip: Reason for listening When the students first listen to the dialogue with their books closed, give them a very general task to do – it gets them used to listening for gist and it makes them concentrate a bit harder!

- Ask students to cover the dialogue. Say: *Listen. How many people do you hear?* (Four – Anna, Susan, Tom, Dave) Play ▶ 1/2.
- Ask students to look at the photo. Ask: *Where are they?* (In the family history class / in a college.) Say: *Now look at the dialogue and listen to it again.* Play the dialogue ▶ 1/2 a second time.

Language and culture

In every step, there's a reference to the *Language and culture* section at the end of the unit. The students can read these texts and do the related tasks at home. There's a key to the tasks in the coursebook. However, if you have extra time at the end of the lesson, you could look at the relevant *L&C* in class. The first *L&C* focusses on Anna's home town, *Ottawa* (coursebook p. 25). For more information on this, look at page 80 of this TRB.

1a How to say it: Introductions and greetings
5– mins

1c), 2d), 3b), 4a)

1b Now you: Introducing each other
5 mins

NB: The *Now you* exercises appear in each step. They give students the opportunity to personalise the language items they have just learnt.

- Demonstrate the activity by introducing one of your students to the rest of the class.

1c Comprehension
10– mins

Tip: Task complexity (1) When you see an arrow like this ↓, there's a suggestion how to make the activity a little easier. When you see this arrow ↑, there's a suggestion how to make the activity a bit more demanding. These suggestions are optional – it depends on the ability of your group whether you choose to use them or not.

- ↓ Students work in pairs and work out the answers before they are read out in class.

1 ~~are~~ / aren't, 2 is / ~~isn't~~, 3 are / ~~aren't~~, 4 ~~is~~ / isn't, 5 is / ~~isn't~~, 6 is / ~~isn't~~

2a Vocabulary: Hobbies and interests
1/3
5+ mins

Tip: Knowing what to listen for When students have to listen for information, always give them time to read through the instructions or questions before they listen so they know what information they should listen out for.

- ↓ Divide the class into three groups. Each group focusses on just one list. Play ▶ 1/3. Answers are shared in class and, if necessary, play ▶ 1/3 again so students can check their answers.

✓ cooking, classical music, films, history

> **Dave:** OK, let's begin. Welcome to the class. I see we have one or two new students – one from Canada! So let's introduce ourselves. I'm Dave – Dave Evans. I'm from Canterbury originally and I'm the director of the museum here in Faversham. Shall we say a bit about our hobbies, too? Well, I like cooking. I love Italian food! And I like Italian music, too – opera, and ... well, all classical music, really. Er ... I love films and I go to the cinema nearly every week. And, of course, I'm interested in history – it's my job and my hobby. That's all really. So, who's next? How about one of our new students ...

2b Now you: Your hobbies
5 mins

- Monitor the activity, giving help with vocabulary where necessary.

3 How to say it: Asking about words
5 mins

- Have the class repeat the phrases after you in chorus.

3a What are these things?
5+ mins

! BE: mobile phone; AE: cell phone
! Write *comb* on the board and practise the pronunciation (silent *b*). Board: comb

1 pen, 2 passport, 3 lipstick, 4 mobile phone, 5 brush, 6 newspaper, 7 key, 8 comb

3b Now you: Your things
5+ mins

- Demonstrate the activity by producing three things from your bag and writing the names of them on the board.

4 Grammar
5 mins

NB: The Grammar section is often divided into two parts: The *You already know* section and the *And now* section. *You already know* focusses on grammar which students should have come across in Starter courses (or earlier in the book) and it's used as a stepping stone to the new grammar which is introduced in the lesson – the *And now* grammar.

You already know: *it's* and *they're*
And now: *this*, *that*, *these* and *those*

- Demonstrate *this* (singular + near) and *these* (plural + near) by touching and naming objects in the classroom. Demonstrate *that* (singular + distant) and *those* (plural + distant) by pointing to and naming objects in the classroom.

4a Remember the sentences
5+ mins

- Let students decide whether they want to refer to the dialogue or not.

1 those, that; 2 this; 3 that, that; 4 these

If short of time

If you notice you're getting short of time,
- do ***Exercise 4b*** as a class activity. Ask students to take an item from their bags and put it on their desk. Walk around, point to an item and elicit:
  That's (Peter's passport). / Those are (Petra's keys).
- do just one of the ***Round up*** activities.

4b What's in your bag?
5+ mins

- Demonstrate the activity by taking a pen out of your bag and asking a student: *Excuse me, what's this in English?* (Elicit: That's a pen.) Take two books out of your bag and ask a student: *Excuse me, what are these in English?* (Elicit: Those are books.)

Round up

NB: The *Round up* activities consolidate the structures which were introduced in the lesson. They also facilitate time flexibility at the end of the lesson.

5a Find out about your partner
5– mins

Tip: Demonstrations It's advisable to demonstrate the activities so that students have a pattern to base their answers / conversations on and, if necessary, write a few keywords on the board.

- Demonstrate the activity by saying a few sentences about yourself.

5b Introduce your partner to the class
5– mins

- Follow coursebook instructions.

And finally ...
5+ mins

Students can only make the most of their course if they're familiar with what their coursebook has to offer. Gradually introduce them to the different possibilities to reinforce what they've learnt. Point out the following features of the coursebook and give a short explanation:
- **Language study** (p. 12): An overview of the grammar in the step – the *You already know* is revision grammar, the *And now* is the grammar that is introduced in the step.
- **Selfstudy** (p. 13): Students can do this in the book or online.
- **Keys** (p. 127) to the Language study and Selfstudy exercises.
- **Language and culture**, Step 1: *Ottawa* and the corresponding task (p. 25).

Tip: You already know – or do you? Less confident students may want extra practice with the *You already know* grammar, that is, the grammar which is assumed knowledge from Starter level in order to go into an A1.2 course, or the grammar which they have come across earlier in this book (applies to the *You already know grammar* in Units 5 and 6). They can practise this grammar by doing the *You already know* exercises on the Language study pages in their book or online – tell them to go to www.langenscheidt.de/networknow/selfstudy and type in the Language study code which is given at the top of each Language study page in *Network Now A1*. Online they find – in addition to the exercises from their book – extra practice of the *You already know* grammar from *Network Now A1 Starter.*

Unit 1 Step 2 In the break

Contents

Storyline	Susan and Anna talk about their jobs and Dave invites them to Faversham museum.
Functions	Likes and dislikes
Vocabulary	Jobs and occupations (1)
Pronunciation	Stressed syllables
Grammar	**You already know:** Pronouns – singular **And now:** Pronouns – plural

Lesson notes

Additional material

For optional and additional material for Unit 1, Step 2, see pages 80/81.
Refer to this section before your lesson as some of the materials require preparation.

Optional stages

Optional stages of the lesson are written in grey in these notes.

**Starter:
What's the word?**
5 mins

NB: Students will have more chance to practise the alphabet in Step 3, so you needn't spend too long on the alphabet – but you may want to remind them of the vowels.
Write on the board: A-team email iPhone O2 YouTube and have students repeat them.

- Spell some words from Step 1, e.g. *seat*, *move*, *down*, *meet*, *Canadian*, *introduce*, *pleased*, *year*.
- ↑ When someone has guessed the word, ask a volunteer to put it into a sentence.

What's your job?
1/8
5 mins

- Ask students to cover the dialogue and listen so that they can add names to the sentences on the board.
  Board:

________	is a computer programmer.	(Anna)
________	works in a hotel.	(Susan)
________	was an engineer.	(Tom)
________	is a museum director.	(Dave)

- Play ▶ 1/8. Students listen to the dialogue with the dialogue covered, and a second time with the dialogue uncovered so they can check their answers.

Language and culture

The students can read the text *Canterbury* (p. 25) and do the related tasks at home – or you can use this as a 'filler' if you have time at the end of the lesson. For more information on this, look at page 81 of this TRB.

1a Comprehension
5 mins

- Students do the exercise alone and then compare answers in class and correct the false statements.
  True: 1, 4, 6
  2 Anna works in ~~Faversham~~ **Canterbury.** 3 Susan's job ~~isn't interesting~~ **is really interesting.**
  5 Dave's a ~~computer programmer~~ **museum director.**

1b Vocabulary: Jobs
5 mins

! In English-speaking countries, people are much more vague about their job descriptions when having social conversations: ***I*** *work for (Siemens)* or ***I*** *work in an (IT) department* is sufficient information.

- Students match the halves of sentences and compare answers in class.
  1b), 2a), 3d), 4f), 5g), 6c), 7e)

1c Other people's jobs
10– mins

- Point out the ***Info box*** to remind students that *a / an* is needed when they say what their job is. Ask *What's Anna's job?* (She's a computer programmer.) *What was Tom's job?* (He was an engineer.)

2 Say it like this
1/9–10
5 mins

- Play ▶ 1/9 so that students can underline the stressed syllables.

<u>doc</u>tor, elec<u>tri</u>cian, <u>fa</u>mily, ho<u>tel</u>, <u>in</u>teresting, <u>mu</u>sic, <u>prob</u>lem, <u>stu</u>dent, <u>tour</u>ist
- Play ▶ 1/10 so that students get a chance to practise the pronunciation.

Tip: Choral repetition Don't be inhibited about asking the whole class to repeat phrases together. This gives every student a chance to practise the phrases. And it allows more hesitant students to practise speaking without doing it in front of the class.

3 Grammar
5+ mins

You already know: Singular pronouns – *my*, *me*, etc.
And now: Plural pronouns – *our*, *us*, etc.

- Read out the sentences and have the class repeat them in chorus.

3a Listening: Where's class 3c?
1/11–12
5+ mins

- First ask the class to speculate: *Look at the photo. They're new students. What's their problem, do you think?*
- Say: *Now listen and find out.* Play ▶ 1/11.

They can't find their classroom.
- Say: *Listen again. What do they say? Coose the right word in number 1–6.* Play ▶ 1/12.
1 our, 2 their, 3 us, 4 we, 5 They're, 6 them

(S1 = Student 1, S2 = Student 2, D = Dave)
S1: Oh no. Where's our classroom?
S2: I don't know. It's classroom 3c. Is that 3c?
S1: No, that's 3f – it's a German class. We can ask their teacher.
S2: Can *she* help us?
S1: Well, we can ask her.
S2: No, look – they're busy. They're in the middle of a lesson. Don't disturb them.
S1: Ah, look, ... here's 3c!
D: Hello. Come in. Welcome to the class!

3b Walk and talk
5+ mins

Tip: Walk and talk Students who are new to the *Network Now* series may not be used to standing up and walking around during the lesson. But moving around not only refreshes the student (many of whom have had a long working day behind them) but it also gives students the opportunity to speak to several people in the class, not just their neighbours on the right and on the left. – Take part in these activities yourself – it helps you to get to know your students and it can help to break down inhibitions on the students' part.

- Demonstrate the activity by writing *my* on a piece of paper and asking two or three able students to make a sentence with that word.

4 How to say it: Likes and dislikes
5 mins

- Have students repeat the phrases chorally. Exaggerate the intonation slightly so that they can copy it easily.
- Ask volunteers to make sentences replacing *it* with a person or a thing. Demonstrate the activity by making sentences with the phrases from the first box, e.g.
I like <u>English</u> very much.
I love <u>my cat</u>.
I think <u>Harry Potter</u> is great.

4a Now you: Do you like it?
5+ mins

- Demonstrate the activity by talking about your home town for a minute.

If short of time	If you notice you're getting short of time, • do ***Exercise 4b*** as a class activity. • do just one of the ***Round up*** activities.
4b Now you: What do you think of it? 10 mins	• Refer them to the phrases in *Exercise 4* before they work with a partner. • ↑ Invite students to add some more items to the list.
Round up **5a Jobs** 5– mins	• Follow coursebook instructions. **Anna works for Silver Star, in Canterbury. She's a computer programmer. Dave is the director of the museum in Faversham. Susan works in a hotel in the town centre. Tom is retired. He was an engineer.**
5b Likes and dislikes 10 mins	• Demonstrate the activity by writing three sentences on the board: I really like (English). I love (cats). I can't stand (jazz). • Students guess which sentence is false and then do the activity in pairs.
And finally ... 5+ mins	Remind students of the following: • **Language study** (p. 16): An overview of the grammar of the step (both *You already know* and *And now*). • **Selfstudy** (p. 17): Students can do this in the book or online. • **Keys** (p. 127) to the Language study and Selfstudy exercises. • **Language and culture**, Step 2: *Canterbury* and the corresponding tasks (p. 25). Encourage students to do the Internet task at home. And point out ... • the **Lerntipp** on pronunciation at the end of the Selfstudy page (p. 17).

Unit 1 Step 3 At the airport

Contents

Realia	A landing card; Airport signs
Functions	Giving personal information; Filling in a form
Vocabulary	Email addresses; Airport signs; BE and AE
Reading	Lost property
Grammar	*Whose …?*; Genitive *'s*

Lesson notes

Additional material

For optional and additional material for Unit 1, Step 3, see pages 81/82.
Refer to this section before your lesson as some of the materials require preparation.

Optional stages

Optional stages of the lesson are written in grey in these notes.

Starter: Can you spell your name, please?
5 mins

! Students often have problems with the alphabet so it's a good idea to have the students practise the alphabet before doing the tasks. Simply have them say the alphabet a couple of times round the class. The 'problem' letters for German speakers are usually:
A R E I G J H V W Y

Tip: Network Teachers' Club The alphabet needs to be practised regularly. For ideas on how to do this, go to the *Network Teachers' Club* (www.langenscheidt.de/network/club; 'January 2010', 'Network lesson: The alphabet (A1.1)').

Forms
1a All about Anna
5+ mins

NB: In the third steps, there's always a piece of realia as a main focus. It's important that students realise that, although there may be unknown words in a text, they shouldn't panic! They will still probably be able to understand enough to cope with the situation.

- Read the ***Info box*** to your class and assure them that it isn't always necessary to understand every word of a text or a conversation – they can still cope in everyday situations.
- Students work alone and then compare answers in class.
  ✓ 1, 3, 6

Language and culture

The students can read the text *Titles* (p. 25) and do the related tasks at home – or you can use this as a 'filler' if you have time at the end of the lesson. For more information on this, look at page 82 of this TRB.

1b Personal details
5+ mins

! Point out: *Where were you born?* (**not** *Where are you born?*)
- Students match the formal headings to the informal questions.
  1e), 2a), 3b), 4c), 5d)

1c Now you: Your personal details
5 mins

- Follow coursebook instructions.

Email addresses
2a How to say it
1/18
5– mins

- Play ▶ 1/18 and refer students to the phrases in the blue box.

(A = Anna, O = Official)
O: … and can I have your email address, please?
A: Yes – it's annaturner, all one word, @ silverstar.com.
O: Sorry, can you spell your name, please?
A: Yes, A-N-N-A-T-U-R-N-E-R
O: annaturner@silverstar.com – right?
A: Yes, that's right.
O: Thank you, Ms Turner. And now can you tell me …?

2b Listening
1/19
5– mins

- Play ▶ T1/19 and students complete the email addresses.

1 jk. 2 @ 3 .uk

1 jk.masters@hobbyenglish.de 2 robert.roy@gfx.ch 3 hg.croft@playtime.co.**uk**

2c Now you: Your email address
5– mins

! Point out the second ***Info box*** in case any student needs this additional information (underscore, dash) to give their own email address.

The airport
3 Airport signs
5+ mins

- Students work alone or in pairs to match the German and English words to the icons.

1 Departures, Abflug; 2 Arrivals, Ankunft; 3 Baggage Claim, Gepäck; 4 Lost Property, Fundsachen; 5 Customs, Zoll

4 Reading: Lost property
10– mins

NB: Students shouldn't be asked to read this text aloud. They don't have to worry about pronunciation of new words – nor is it necessary for them to understand every word. The aim is to get the gist of a text and to guess new words from their context.

Tip: Pre-reading In order to introduce the topic and some of the vocabulary in a reading text, you can ask some speculative questions before reading the text. Don't correct the answers, just let students guess – they'll find out the answers when they read the text. Say: *What do people sometimes lose at airports?* (Bags, umbrellas, phones, etc.) *Let's find out the answers by reading the 'Lost Property' text, Exercise 4.*

- Allow students time to read the text silently.
- Ask: *How many airports are there in London?* (Five) *What's the main airport in London?* (Heathrow) *How many passengers travel to or from Heathrow every year?* (68 million)

4a American words
5 mins

! Reassure students that British English and American English are very similar but there are sometimes differences. In dictionaries, *BE* indicates British English and *AE* indicates American English. These terms are used in *Exercise 4* on the *Selfstudy* page (p. 20).

- Students find the corresponding British word in the text and check their answers by reading out the sentence from the text.
  1 luggage, 2 mobile phones, 3 handbags

If short of time

If you notice you're getting short of time,
- do ***Exercise 4b*** as a class activity.
- limit the number of items in ***Exercise 5b***.

4b Listening
1/20
5 mins

- Play ▶ 1/20.

1 passport, 2 keys, 3 bag

1 (CO = Customs Official, A = Anna, W = Woman) CO: Can I see your passport, please? A: Yes, it's here – in my bag. Oh, where is it? W: Excuse me – are you Anna Turner? A: Yes, that's right. What ...? W: Is *this* your passport? A: Oh yes, it is. Thank you so much. Where was it? W: It was on the desk at ...

→

2 (S = Simon, G1 = Girl, D = Dave)
S: Look – there are some keys on that table. Whose keys are they, do you know?
G1: No. Dave.
D: Yes?
G1: These keys were on the table in your classroom.
D: Oh yes – they're my keys. My car keys. Thanks very much.
G1: It's OK, Simon – they're Dave's keys.

3 (G2 = Girl, S = Susan)
G2: Dave.
D: Yes?
G2: Is this *your* bag?
D: Pardon?
G2: Is this your bag?
D: No, it isn't.
G2: It was on the chair in the café. Whose bag is it, do you know?
D: No – but look inside, maybe there's a name in it.
G2: OK ... Yes, here's a card Ms S Davis.
D: Oh, that's Susan. It's her bag. Susan, is this your bag?
S: Oh yes, it is. Thanks.
G2: It was in the café. It was on the chair and I ...

5 Grammar
5– mins

NB: There is only a minor grammar element in the third steps – the main focus is on realia and reading.

Whose ... is it? / Whose ... are they? – It's ...'s ... / They're ...'s ...

- Read out the sentences in the grammar box and have the class repeat them in chorus.

5a Listening
1/21
10– mins

- Say: *Listen again. Tick the correct information.* Play ▶ 1/21.

1c), 2b), 3b)

Audio script: see above in *Exercise 4b* (pages 15/16)

5b Lost Property Office
10– mins

- Collect items from the students and put them on your table. Keep to items students know – only have a few new things so they're not overwhelmed by new vocabulary.
- Pick up one item and asking: *What's this in English?* to remind them that they can ask you for the names of objects they don't know. Then demonstrate the activity as it's described in the coursebook.

And finally ...
5+ mins

Remind students of the following:
- **Language study** (p. 20): An overview of the grammar of the step.
- **Selfstudy** (p. 20): Students can do this in the book or online.
- **Keys** (p. 127) to the Language study and Selfstudy exercises.
- **Language and culture**, Step 3: *Titles* and the corresponding tasks (p. 25).

And point out ...
- **Reading: At the Lost Property Office** (p. 21): A text 'just for fun' with a glossary of unknown words. For more information on this, look at pages 82 and 119 of this TRB.

Unit 1 Now I can

Contents

Review of vocabulary, functions and structures in Unit 1

Storyline	The *Now I can* pages have their own characters. In Unit 1, we meet Alun, who joins a German class in Canterbury and the students write personal profiles.
Starter	Introducing yourself and others
Part 1	Filling in a form; Asking for and giving personal information
Part 2	Talking and writing about jobs and hobbies; Expressing likes and dislikes
Part 3	Writing about jobs

Lesson notes

Additional material

For optional and additional material for Unit 1, *Now I can*, see page 82.
Refer to this section before your lesson as some of the materials require preparation.

Optional stages

Optional stages of the lesson are written in grey in these notes.

Jetzt kann ich u. a.: ...
5– mins

- Ask students to look at *Jetzt kann ich u. a.: ...* Remind them that the symbols refer to different skills or vocabulary items which they learnt in Unit 1 and were listed in the aims on the photo page (p. 9). Most of the tasks in *Now I can* focus on more than one skill or vocabulary item.

Starter:
The people in Unit 1
10 mins

- Students say what they know about the characters who appeared in Unit 1.

E.g. Anna's from Canada. Her grandparents were from Faversham originally. She works as a computer programmer in Canterbury. Dave teaches the family history course. He's the director of Faversham museum. He likes cooking, Italian food and music / classical music, history and films. Susan works in a hotel. She's married to Tom. She lives in Faversham. Tom is Susan's husband. He was an engineer but he's retired now.

Part 1:
1a Why are they there?
1/25
15 mins

Tip: Task complexity (2) When an exercise can be made easier for the whole class, you see ↓; and ↑ means it can be made more complex. This is a decision the teacher makes for the whole class. Now, for some exercises, we're introducing a system whereby the student can decide for himself / herself how adventurous they want to be! All the class does the same basic exercise, but to varying degrees of complexity, signalled by a star system. It involves your writing 3 short tasks on the board. The first task (*) is easier than in the coursebook; the second task (**) is the standard task as in the coursebook; the third task (***) is more complex than in the coursebook.

Anna wants to find out more about her family. They were from Faversham originally.

- Read the instructions to the class. Give them time to read through the possible reasons for learning German.
- Explain the 'star system' to the class: *Maybe you had a hard day at work today and you're tired? You can do an easier task – a one-star task; most of you can do the task that you read in the coursebook – the two-star task; do you want a challenge (Herausforderung)? Then do the three-star task.*
  Board:
  * Listen for reasons a)–e) or listen for reasons f)–j).
  ** As in the coursebook.
  *** Do **. Then tell the class what the man says about holidays.
- Students listen to why the people are in a German course. Play ▶ 1/25.
- Play the conversation a second time ▶ 1/25 so students can check their answers.
  a), c), e), f), g), h), i), j)

(A–F = a group of adult students)
A: What are your reasons for doing this course? For me – it's just a hobby, I love learning ... but I'm sure it isn't a hobby for you all.
B: No, for me – it isn't a hobby. It's important for my job.
A: Oh? What do you do?
B: I work in a travel office and I often phone our partners in Germany. They speak good English but I want to learn to speak good German.
C: Well, I love skiing so I'd like to go to Switzerland or Austria for a winter holiday next year. I know that people speak good English there but I'd like to speak a bit of German, too! That's why *I'm* here.
B: Did you learn German at school?
C: Yes, I *did* – but my German from my schooldays is bad – and we didn't speak very much. What about you?
D: Well, I just *like* German. It's an interesting language.
E: Oh, please tell my children that. They always have problems with their homework – and they always ask me for help!
F: Well, I come to the course for two reasons. First of all, I work at home on a computer *all* day. I never talk to other people. So, it's really good to come to this course and talk to you ... in German or English. And I enjoy the time in the pub with you after the lesson, too.
E: And the second reason?
F: I think I want to do an examination in German.
E: Oh, why?
F: I don't really know why ... I just want to see my level, I think.
E: Yes ... that's a good idea. Perhaps we could ask the teacher about the examinations that we can ...

- Students then talk in groups about why they are in an English course. Monitor this activity, showing interest and prompting shy students.
  NB: Ask: *Why are you on an English course?* or *Why do you want to learn English?* or *What are your reasons for doing this course?* (Not: *Why are you learning English?* The present progressive is introduced in *Network Now A2.1.*)
- Ask individual students to tell the class why they are in the English course.

1b The new student

1/26
10 mins

- Students listen and complete a form about Alun, a new student. Play ▶ 1/26.

Family name: **Burton**; First name(s): **Alun**; Date of birth: -; Nationality: **British**; Address: **3 London Road, Canterbury, CT3 6SG**; Contact tel.: **079 413 465 83**; Email: **alunburton@gmx.co.uk**; Course title: **German A2**; Course number: **215**; Day and time: **Tuesdays, 7pm**

- Play the dialogue a second time ▶ 1/26 so that students can check their answers.

(A = Alun, R = School Receptionist)
R: Good evening – can I help you?
A: Yes, I'm here for the German course.
R: Oh right. Erm, I just need some details from you. Can you tell me your first name please?
A: Yes, it's Alun ... that's A L *U* N.
R: Oh, that's interesting.
A: Yes, my parents were from Wales, from Cardiff. And A L U N is the Welsh way to spell Alan.
R: So, you're British.
A: Yes, I am. But why do you ask that?
R: It's just for our statistics – here in the school. That's all.
A: Oh, I see.
R: And what's your family name?
A: Burton. B U R T O N.
R: B U R T O N ... thanks. And can I have your address, please?
A: Yes, it's 3 London Road ...
R: Yes ...
A: Canterbury – CT3 6SG.

R: CT3 6SG ... thank you. And could I have a contact telephone number and perhaps an email address for you?
A: Is a mobile number OK?
R: Yes, of course.
A: It's 079
R: 079
A: 413 ... 465 ... 83
R: 079 413 465 83.
A: Yes, that's right. And my email address is alunburton, all one word, at gmx.co.uk.
R: OK, alunburton at gmx.co.uk. Right ... thanks very much. And your course is ...?
A: German A2.
R: OK, that's course number ... let me see ... 215. On Tuesdays at 7 o'clock. Yes, well, it's ten to seven now so you can go to the room – it's room number 18 on the first floor.
A: Good – thanks very much.
R: Enjoy your lesson.

1c Role play
10+ mins

- Follow coursebook instructions.
  NB: The one piece of information which Alun wasn't asked was his date of birth. Remind students that the question is: *When were you born?* And also remind them that they needn't give true answers!

Part 2:
2a We want to know you better!
5 mins

- Students read Alun's profile. Then ask: *Who has something in common with Alun?*
  Board: Alun ________________ and I ________________, too.

2b Your personal profile
10 mins

- Before students do the writing activity, ask individual students: *What can you say about your ...* (choose one of the categories).

2c Show a partner
10 mins

Tip: Pairwork (1) Encourage your students to work with a variety of partners – it makes it more interesting for them to get to know each other better, and it's also good practice to hear English from different speakers. If they're reluctant to change partners or move from their seats, say: *Work with a student who has something in common with you. (Arbeiten Sie mit einem Kursteilnehmer / einer Kursteilnehmerin zusammen, die etwas mit Ihnen gemeinsam hat.): Who has a birthday in October?* (When students put their hands up, pair them off.) *Who has a white car? Who has a grandchild? Who has a nice boss? Who has two mobile phones? Who has a cat? Who has ...?*

- Follow coursebook instructions.

If short of time

The **final activity** of the *Now I can* pages allows for time flexibility as it's often an open-ended activity. Students can interview their teacher, rather than writing a text.

Part 3:
Our teacher's job
10 mins

- Students read the description of Alun's job silently.
- Students ask the teacher for information.
- ↓ Ask individual students a question and then have them answer it and ask you the same question: Teacher: *What do you do?*
  Student: *I'm a ... And you? What do you do?*
  Teacher: ...
  Where do you work? When do you work? Do you work at the weekends? Do you like your job?
- Students write a profile of their teacher's job, based on the information they got from the teacher.

And finally ...
5 mins

Point out the following features of the coursebook and give a short explanation:

- **Test yourself** (p. 24): Students can assess their progress by doing this test and checking their answers (p. 127).
- **Language and culture** (p. 25): Refer your students to any *L&C* texts and tasks that weren't read or done in class.
- **Now me** (p. 26): Students have the opportunity to personalise the structures they learnt in the previous unit and practise writing English. Advise them to keep a record of their progress by assembling a dossier. Refer them to www.langenscheidt.de/networknow/portfolio.

Unit 2 Step 1 Weekdays

Contents

Storyline Anna and Susan talk about their daily routines.
Functions Talking about routines; Telling the time
Vocabulary Jobs and workplaces (2)
Grammar **You already know:** Present simple
And now: Adverbs of frequency *(always, usually, often, sometimes, never)*

Lesson notes

Additional material
For optional and additional material for Unit 2, Step 1, see pages 82/83. Refer to this section before your lesson as some of the materials require preparation.

Optional stages
Optional stages of the lesson are written in grey in these notes.

Photo page
5– mins

- Students look at the photos on page 27 and answer the questions.

  Anna works in (a)) an office; Susan goes (b)) swimming.
- Refer students to *In dieser Unit lernen Sie u. a.: ...* and give them time to read about what they're going to learn in Unit 2.

Starter: Routines
5– mins

Demonstrate the activity by telling the students something that you do every day / once a week. Then they have a pattern to say what they do every day / once a week.

My day
1/29
5+ mins

- Board: ______________ starts work early. (Anna)
- Ask stu dents to cover the dialogue. Refer students to the board and ask: *Is that Anna or Susan?* Play ▶ 1/29.
- Play ▶ 1/29 again so that students can check the answer.

Language and culture
The students can read the text *Time* (p. 43) and do the related task at home – or you can use this as a 'filler' if you have time at the end of the lesson. For more information on this, look at page 83 of this TRB.

1a Comprehension
5 mins

- Students put Anna's daily routines in the right order.

  left column: 2, 5, 3; right column: 1, 4
- ↑ Ask individual students to say three things about their morning routine.

1b Times
5+ mins

! Remind students that *am* (ante meridiem) is used for the times midnight to midday (0–12) and that *pm* is used for the times from midday to midnight (12–24).
- Students underline the times in the dialogue and individuals read them out.
  eight o'clock, quarter past six, twenty past seven, quarter to ten, half past eight
- Ask volunteers to read out the sentences which contain the times.

2 How to say it: Telling the time
5+ mins

- Have the class repeat the times in chorus.
- Point out the ***Info box*** and practise the half hour by writing a few times on the board (7.30 – 4.30 – 1.30, etc.) and asking individuals to say them.

2a What's the time?
5 mins

- ↓ First do this as a class activity: *Student A, ask Student B about number (4).* Choose the weaker students to ask the question for the first few examples.
- Students work in pairs, ask each other the time and give the answers.
  1 It's eleven o'clock. 2 It's quarter past three. 3 It's twenty-five past four. 4 It's twenty to nine. 5 It's half past one. 6 It's twenty-five to one.

! During the lesson, ask individual students: *What's the time?*

2b Now you: What do you do when?
10– mins

- Demonstrate the activity by writing the time of one of your routines on the board and getting the class to guess what you do.
- Students work in pairs and ask each other about their daily routines.

3 Grammar
5 mins

You already know: Present simple
! If some of your students are not very confident and want more revision practice, refer them to the *You already know* section of the *Language study* (p. 30). They can do the exercises in their book or online – tell them to go to www.langenscheidt.de/networknow/selfstudy and type in the Language study code which is given at the top of page 30. Online they find – in addition to the exercises from their book – extra practice of the *You already know* grammar from *Network Now A1 Starter.*

And now: Adverbs of frequency *(always, usually, often, sometimes, never)*
! Students will need practice in pronouncing the word *usually.*
- Have the class repeat the phrases after you in chorus.

3a Now you: Your day
10– mins

- Students write in the adverbs of frequency to make the sentences true for them.
- Check answers in class. Students ask questions with *How often do you ...?*, eliciting the sentences which were written down.
- ↓ Practise the 3rd person singular by asking individuals to read sentences 1–7 beginning with *My best friend ...*

Tip: Correction (1) Write the letter ***S*** on a card – or on the palm of your hand – and, when students forget to add an *-s* on the verb when talking about the third person, simply hold up the card / your hand – this avoids having to interrupt them to get them to correct the mistake.

3b How often do you ...?
5+ mins

! Remind students that the single 'how often' words go before the main verb:
Board: I often go there ,
but the 'how often' phrases go at the end of the sentence:
Board: I go there every week.
- ↓ Ask individual students to replace the underlined words on the board with alternatives.
- Let students work in pairs for five minutes and then report one fact about their partner to the class. (Keep that *S*-card handy!)

If short of time

If you notice you're getting short of time,
- just have them give only one possible answer in ***Exercise 4a***.
- do just one of the ***Round up*** activities.

4a Vocabulary: Jobs and workplaces
5+ mins

- Do this as a class activity.
  ! Check the stress in the words: electrician, engineer, assistant, receptionist.

  Possible answers: **hotel – cleaner, cook, manager, receptionist, waiter; shop – manager, shop assistant; school – cleaner, teacher; house – babysitter, cleaner, electrician, housewife, cook; restaurant – cleaner, cook, manager, waiter; hospital – cleaner, cook, doctor, nurse, receptionist; factory – electrician, engineer, factory worker, manager; office – cleaner, engineer, manager, PA, receptionist**

4b Routines
1/30–31
5+ mins

- Play ▶ 1/30 so students can identify the three people's jobs.

  1 waiter, 2 shop assistant, 3 nurse
- Play ▶ 1/31 so students can note down the details.

Speaker 1: ~~sometimes~~, ~~never~~; ~~always~~, ~~usually~~;
Speaker 2: sometimes, always;
Speaker 3: He often works at night. First / At about 6pm he always has a meeting with the doctors. He usually walks round and talks to the patients. He's sometimes really tired. He never sleeps well in the day. He's never bored.

1 I enjoy my job but the working hours aren't great. I often work till after midnight. You see, people come to the restaurant for dinner – usually around 8 or 9 o'clock, have dinner, then they order more drinks, then they want coffee ... The last person usually leaves around midnight – and, of course, I can't go home before they leave. But the positive thing is – I don't get up before ten o'clock in the morning. I get to the restaurant before lunch so I can prepare ...

2 I work in a small shoe shop in town. I sell men's shoes. My job's OK – but I don't like my boss! And I don't think he likes me. You see, the shop opens at nine and I – well, I have problems getting up in the morning so I'm sometimes late for work. I work from nine to six – it's a really long day. And weekends, too! But I always have a day off in the week. And then *I* go shopping!

3 I work in a hospital and people always think I'm a doctor, but I'm not. The hospital is a hectic place in the day but I often work at night, when it's nice and quiet. I start work at about 6 pm and first we always have a meeting with the doctors. Then I usually walk round and talk to the patients. Working at night can be hard. I'm sometimes really tired when I finish work and I never sleep very well in the day – but, yes, I like my job and I'm never bored.

Round up
5a Routines at work
5– mins

- Use the jobs in *Exercise 4a* as prompts.

5b An interview
5– mins

- Demonstrate the activity by inviting students to ask you questions before they work with a partner.

And finally ...
5+ mins

Remind students of the following:

- **Language study** (p. 30): Students can do this in their book or online – tell them to go to www.langenscheidt.de/networknow/selfstudy and type in the Language study code which is given at the top of page 30. Online they find – in addition to the exercises from their book – extra practice of the *You already know* grammar from *Network Now A1 Starter.*
- **Selfstudy** (p. 31): Students can do this in the book or online.
- **Keys** (p. 127 / 128) to the Language study and Selfstudy exercises.
- **Language and culture,** Step 1: *Time* and the corresponding task (p. 43).

Unit 2 Step 2 Weekends

Contents

Storyline Anna and Susan talk about their free time.
Functions Making and reacting to suggestions
Vocabulary Positive and negative adjectives
Pronunciation Intonation: Returning questions *(And you? What did you do?)*
Grammar **You already know:** Questions
And now: More questions (*Why …? – Because …*; prepositions at the end of questions, e.g. *Which part of London do you live in?)*

Lesson notes

Additional material
For optional and additional material for Unit 2, Step 2, see page 83.
Refer to this section before your lesson as some of the materials require preparation.

Optional stages
Optional stages of the lesson are written in grey in these notes.

Starter: How often?
5– mins

- ↓ Before students open their books, remind them of 'how often' words, before doing the task.
  Board: always, never, often, sometimes, usually
  Ask students to write these 'how often' words in their notebooks in the order of frequency, beginning with: *always (usually, often, sometimes, never).*
- Ask two students to read the example sentences.
- Demonstrate the activity by telling the students something that you remember about someone in the class. Then invite students to do the same.

After class
1/35
5+ mins

- Ask students to cover the dialogue. Refer students to the board and say: *Listen to Anna and Susan. What are the missing names?* Play ▶ 1/35.
  Board:
  1 ____________ likes cooking.
  2 ____________ wants to go to London at the weekend.
- Play ▶ 1/35 again so that students can check their answers. (1 Tom, 2 Anna)

Language and culture
The students can read the text *Free time* (p. 43) and do the related tasks at home – or you can use this as a 'filler' if you have time at the end of the lesson. For more information on this, look at page 83 of this TRB.

1a Comprehension
5 mins

- Students answer the questions in class.

1 They often invite friends to their place for dinner. 2 Because she wants to visit Mrs Benton. 3 She's an old family friend. 4 She went to school with Anna's grandmother.

1b Vocabulary: Adjectives
5+ mins

Tip: Terminology Students are sometimes unnerved by grammatical terms, so don't overuse them. In *Exercise 1b*, simply say: *Adjectives – words that tell us about things and people* – and then read out the list in *Exercise 1b* as examples.

- Students distinguish between positive and negative adjectives and make sentences using adjectives.
  Positive: fantastic, good, great, interesting; Negative: awful, boring, difficult, terrible
- ↑ Volunteers can make their own sentences, without using prompts from the book.

2 How to say it: Making and reacting to suggestions
5+ mins

- Read out the list of suggestions and have the class repeat them in chorus.
- Ask volunteers to find and read out the suggestions used in the text. (How about coming to dinner …? Why don't we have dinner together …?)
- Read out the list of reactions to suggestions and have the class repeat them in chorus.
- Ask volunteers to find and read out Anna's reactions to the suggestions. (I'm sorry, I can't. I'd love to – thanks.)

2a After the lesson
1/36–37
10– mins

- Play ▶ 1/36 and a volunteer gives the answer.

They decide to go for an Indian meal.
- Go around the class, saying *A* or *B* alternately to each student (this saves discussion time!). They then do the task.
- Play ▶ 1/37.
A: ✓ e), b), a), d); B: ✓ a), b), d)

> (A = Anna, D = Dave, J = Jenny)
> A: Bye Dave. See you next Tuesday.
> D: Bye you two. Have a good evening.
> A: Shall we go for a drink, Jenny? Do you have time?
> J: I'd love to – but I'm hungry, too. I didn't have lunch today. How about going for a pizza?
> A: Hmm, we could – or we could go for an Indian meal ...
> J: Oh yes, an Indian meal. Good idea! I love Indian food. Let's go to that new Indian restaurant in King Street.
> A: That sounds great!

2b Now you: What shall we do?
5+ mins

- Demonstrate the activity by making suggestions to different students and eliciting a response: *Shall we go to the opera at the weekend? What about a rock concert?*
- Students react to suggestions about what to do after the lesson and then report to the class.

3 Grammar
5 mins

You already know: Questions
! If some of your students are not very confident and want more revision practice, refer them to the *You already know* section of the *Language study* (p. 34). They can do the exercises in their book or online – tell them to go to www.langenscheidt.de/networknow/selfstudy and type in the Language study code which is given at the top of page 34. Online they find – in addition to the exercises from their book – extra practice of the *You already know* grammar from *Network Now A1 Starter.*

And now: More questions (*Why ...? – Because ...*; prepositions at the end of questions, e.g. *Which house does she live in?)*
- Have the class read the questions in the *You already know* box. Ask: *We don't know the answer to one question here. Which question is it?* (How often does Anna go to London?)
- In pairs, students ask and answer the other five questions. (Mrs Benton is an old family friend. She must be nearly ninety. She lives in London. The lesson (i.e. your lesson) starts at ... Anna can have dinner with Susan and Tom on Monday evening.)
- Read out the sentences in the *And now* box and have students repeat them in chorus.

3a Questions
10– mins

- Remind students of the star system (see Unit 1 *Now I can*, p. 17) and write the options for doing the first part of *Exercise 3a* on the board.
Board:

*	Work in pairs.
**	Do the task alone.
***	Do ** and then write a similar question.

If a student has chosen the 3-star option, invite him / her to write the question on the board and choose a student to read out the question with the correct question word.
- Students choose the right question word.
1 Why, 2 Who, 3 What, 4 Where, 5 When, 6 What time, 7 Why
- Students (↓ work in pairs) and match the answers to the questions.
3a), 1b), 4c), 6d), 5e), 7f), 2g)

3b Now you: Tell your partner about you
5+ mins

- Follow coursebook instructions.

3c Where do you come from?
5+ mins

! Explain that when you make questions in English, the prepositions, the little words *for, in, from,* etc. go at the end of the question.
Board:
Which part of London does she live <u>in</u>?
- Students complete the questions with a preposition.
  NB: They don't answer the questions yet – first in *Exercise 4b*.
  1 from, 2 to, 3 in, 4 for, 5 to

If short of time

If you notice you're getting short of time,
- do ***Exercise 4b*** as a class activity.
- do just one of the ***Round up*** activities.

4a Say it like this
1/38–39
5+ mins

- Play ▶ 1/38.

Where do you come from? I come from Athens. And you? Where do you come from? I come from Bonn.

- Have students repeat the questions, with the stress on *you*: *And <u>you</u>? Where do <u>you</u> come from?*
- Say: *Listen and repeat the questions.* Play ▶ 1/39.

1 Where do you come from? – And you? Where do *you* come from? 2 Which restaurants do you go to? – And you? Which restaurants do *you* go to? 3 What are you interested in? – And you? What are *you* interested in? 4 Which company do you work for? – And you? Which company do *you* work for? 5 What sort of music do you listen to? – And you? What sort of music do *you* listen to?

4b Now you: Walk and talk
5+ mins

- Follow coursebook instructions.

Round up
5a Tell me more
5+ mins

- Demonstrate the activity with an able student by asking him / her: *Do you do a lot of sport? Why ...?*
- This can be done as a walk and talk activity or in groups or in pairs.

5b At the weekend
5– mins

- Demonstrate the activity by inviting students to ask you questions before they work with a partner.

And finally ...
5+ mins

Remind students of the following:
- **Language study** (p. 34): Students can do this in their book or online – tell them to go to <u>www.langenscheidt.de/networknow/selfstudy</u> and type in the Language study code which is given at the top of page 34. Online they find – in addition to the exercises from their book – extra practice of the *You already know* grammar from *Network Now A1 Starter*.
- **Selfstudy** (p. 35): Students can do this in the book or online.
- **Keys** (p. 128) to the Language study and Selfstudy exercises.
- **Language and culture,** Step 2: *Free time* and the corresponding tasks (p. 43). Encourage students to do the Internet task at home.

And point out ...
- the **Lerntipp** on learning vocabulary at the end of the Selfstudy page (p. 35). Refer students to the Unit vocabulary section (pages 150–175) and remind them that they can also listen to the vocabulary lists and phrases. Students can do this by going to <u>www.langenscheidt.de/networknow/selfstudy</u> and typing in the code which is given in the Unit vocabulary (e.g. page 158).

Unit 2 Step 3 At the pub

Contents

Realia	Pub notices; Rules for a pub quiz
Functions	Understanding instructions; Questions
Vocabulary	Pub notices; Quiz rules
Pronunciation	*was / were*
Reading	Molly Malone
Grammar	**You already know:** *How many are there? – There's ... / There are ...* **And now:** *How many were there? – There was ... / There were ...*

Lesson notes

Additional material

For optional and additional material for Unit 2, Step 3, see page 84.
Refer to this section before your lesson as some of the materials require preparation.

Optional stages

Optional stages of the lesson are written in grey in these notes.

Starter:
Where do you go?
5– mins

- Demonstrate the activity by telling the students something about your favourite pub or restaurant.

Pub notices
1a What does it mean?
5+ mins

- Refer the class to the authentic pub signs at the top of the page. Reassure them that they don't need to understand every word – they can often guess the meanings from the context.
- Give the class time to tick the correct information and then invite volunteers to give the answers.
  1a), 2b), 3a), 4b)

Language and culture

The students can read the text *Pubs* (p. 43) and do the related tasks at home – or you can use this as a 'filler' if you have time at the end of the lesson. For more information on this, look at page 84 of this TRB.

Reading: Molly Malone
5 mins

NB: Remember that students aren't expected to read this text aloud, so they are not faced with pronunciation problems initially. And reassure your students that they will hear you read the text in a few minutes.

- Give students time to read the text silently and then ask one or two general questions.
  Where did Molly Malone live? (Dublin) *What did she sell?* (Fish) *Can you see her today?* (Yes – there's a ghost and a statue.)

2a Comprehension
5 mins

- Read the text aloud to the class before asking students to do the task.
  ! Remind them that there is a dictionary at the back of the book if they want to look up a word, but they should try to get the general meaning of the text without needing every single word.
  Dublin, pretty, wheelbarrow, fever, ghost

2b A traditional Irish song
1/44
10 mins

- Students insert the missing words into the song text.

  See key for *Exercise 2a*.
- Play the song ▶ 1/44 so that students can check their answers.
- Play the song again ▶ 1/44 and encourage students to join in.

NB: There's a translation of the words on page 125 of the coursebook. Students can look at this after the lesson.

2c Now you: Songs that you know
5 mins

- Students talk about English songs which are popular in their country.

Tip: Variety If you have students in your class from other countries or other regions, ask them about their home towns. This not only helps them to feel integrated into the class but also adds variety to the answers and information the class hears.

The pub quiz
3a Comprehension
10 mins

FYI: Pubs quizes are a popular form of entertainment in Britain. They are usually held regularly – weekly or monthly. Contestants usually play in teams and answer questions on general knowledge. Prizes usually involve rounds of beer!

- Students read the pub quiz rules silently and then tick the true sentences.
  ✓ 1, 6, 7, 8
- Volunteers then correct the false information.
  2 ... at 8.30, 3 There are two prizes / a first and second prize, 4 ... a maximum of eight people, 5 ... per player

3b Quiz questions
1/45
5 mins

- Students listen and identify the round. Play ▶ 1/45.
- ↓ Board: Music – Sport – General knowledge

General knowledge / First round

(B = Brendan, S = Sandy)
B: It's your quizmaster Brendan with you again for your Tuesday night pub quiz. There are a lot of people here tonight and there's a great atmosphere. How many teams are there tonight, Sandy?
S: There are seven teams tonight, Brendan.
B: Seven teams – great. Last week there were five teams so this week, with seven teams, you must think hard! Good luck. We have five rounds of five questions. Last week there wasn't a music round – sorry. But this week we have all five rounds for you. So now for the first round. Listen and write your answers on your quiz paper.
Question number 1: How many stars are there on the flag of the United States of America? How many stars are there on the US flag?

4 Grammar
5 mins

You already know: *How many are there? – There's ... / There are ...*
! If some of your students are not very confident and want more revision, refer them to the *You already know section* of the Language study (p. 38). They can do it in their book or online – tell them to go to www.langenscheidt.de/networknow/selfstudy and type in the Language study code which is given at the top of page 38. Online they also find extra practice of the *You already know* grammar from *Network Now A1 Starter.*

And now: *How many were there? – There was ... / There were ...*

- Have the class repeat the sentences in the *And now* box.
- Ask volunteers to complete the sentences on the board.
  Board:
  There's a pub quiz this week.
  ________ ________ a pub quiz last week, too.
  There are a lot of teams this week.
  ________ ________ a lot of teams last week, too.

4a Facts about the pub quiz
5 mins

! Students need to use the information from the quiz rules and information they heard in *Exercise 3b.*

- Students choose the correct information and check answers with a partner.
  1 There's, 2 There are, 3 There are, 4 There weren't, 5 There was

4b Say it like this
1/46
5 mins

- Students repeat the sentences, which have a weak pronunciation of *was / were*. Play ▶ 1/46.

1 There were ten teams last week.
2 There wasn't a music round last week.
3 There were a lot of people at the quiz.
4 There was a question about America.
5 There were five music questions.

If short of time

If you notice you're getting short of time,
- do the answering of the questions in ***Exercise 4c*** as a class activity.
- do ***Exercise 4d*** as a class activity by writing just one set of questions (p. 123) and asking individuals to complete a question and ask it to the class.

4c What does Brendan say?
1/47
10 mins

- ↑ Students can try to fill in the questions before listening to the dialogue, and then check their answers by listening.
- Play ▶ 1/47 and students fill in the missing words. In groups, they try to answer the questions.

1 How many; 2 What; 3 many, were there; 4 Who was; 5 Whose
The answers to the questions are on page 125 of the coursebook.

(B = Brendan)
B: Question number 1: How many stars are there on the flag of the United States of America? How many stars are there on the US flag?
And question number 2: Ready? In the name JF Kennedy, what do the initials JF stand for? What do the initials JF stand for in the name JF Kennedy?
Ready for question 3? I know you all remember the Beatles – but how many musicians were there in that pop group? How many musicians were there in the Beatles?
Next is question 4: Who was the first president of the United States of America? Was it a) Abraham Lincoln, b) George Washington, or c) Thomas Jefferson? Who was the first US president?
And question 5, the last question in this round: Whose real name was Clark Kent? That's a bit difficult. Whose real name was Clark Kent?
That's the end of round one. OK Sandy, collect the papers, please. And now for some music. ...

4d Make your own pub quiz
10+ mins

- Divide the class into two teams, A and B, and sit the teams on opposite sides of the room so they can discuss answers within their team.
- Each team chooses a captain to do the writing and make the final decisions.
- Team A looks at page 123; Team B looks at page 125.
- Monitor the activity, giving help where necessary.
- When the captain has filled in the question words, suggested by his / her team, check that they're correct before the questions are asked to the other team.
The question words are the same for both teams: **1 Who, 2 How, 3 When, 4 Whose, 5 Which**

And finally ...
5+ mins

Remind students of the following:
- **Language study** (p. 38): Students can do this in their book or online – tell them to go to www.langenscheidt.de/networknow/selfstudy and type in the Language study code which is given at the top of page 38. Online they find – in addition to the exercises from their book – extra practice of the *You already know* grammar from *Network Now A1 Starter*.
- **Selfstudy** (p. 38): Students can do this in the book or online.
- **Keys** (p. 128) to the Language study and Selfstudy exercises.
- **Language and culture**, Step 3: *Pubs* and the corresponding tasks (p. 43).

And point out ...
Reading: Quiz time – riddles (p. 39): A a text 'just for fun' with a glossary of unknown words. For more information on this, look at pages 84 and 119/120 of this TRB.

Unit 2 Now I can

Contents

Review of vocabulary, functions and structures in Unit 2

Storyline	Some people in Alun's class try to find a time when they can meet.
Starter	Telling the time
Part 1	Understanding rules and instructions; Talking about routines; Asking and answering questions; Talking about jobs
Part 2	Making and reacting to suggestions; Talking about routines
Part 3	Asking and answering questions; Talking about routines

Lesson notes

Additional material

For optional and additional material for Unit 2, *Now I can*, see pages 84/85.
Refer to this section before your lesson as some of the materials require preparation.

Optional stages

Optional stages of the lesson are written in grey in these notes.

Jetzt kann ich u. a.: ...
5– mins

- Ask students to look at *Jetzt kann ich u. a.: ...* Remind them that the symbols refer to different skills or vocabulary items which they learnt in Unit 2 and were listed in the aims on the photo page (p. 27). Most of the tasks in *Now I can* focus on more than one skill or vocabulary item.

Starter:
The times in Unit 2
5+ mins

- Students play a chain game to practise saying the time.

Five past one, ten past one, quarter past one, twenty past one, twenty-five past one, half past one, etc.;
Quarter past seven, half past seven, quarter to eight, eight o'clock, etc.

Part 1:
1a What's my job?
1/52
10+ mins

- Read the instructions to the class. Give them time to read through the four things they have to listen for.
- Remind students of the star system (see Unit 1, *Now I can*, p. 17) and write the options for doing the first part of *Exercise 1a* on the board.
  Board:
*	Do 1, 3 and 4 *or* do 2, 3 and 4.
**	As in the coursebook.
***	Do ** and tell the class two questions that you heard.
- Play ▶ 1/52.
- Play the conversation a second time ▶ 1/52 so students can complete or check their answers.
  1 seven, 2 three, 3 No, it isn't., 4 She works in a travel office. / She's a travel agent.

(A–D = group of four adult students)
A: What's my job?
B: Do you work with children?
A: No, I don't.
C: Do you work inside a building?
A: Yes, I do.
B: Do you work in a hospital?
A: No, I don't.
D: Ah ... I know ... do you work in an office?
A: Yes, I do.
D: I know ... you work in a bank.
A: No, I don't ... sorry.
C: Hhmmm ... Do you phone a lot?
A: Yes, I do.
B: Do you speak other languages in your job?

→

A: Yes, I do.
C: Do you use the Internet a lot?
A: Yes, I do.
B: Do you plan something for people?
A: Yes, I do.
C: I know ... you work in a travel office.
A: Yes, that's right – I plan holidays to Dubai and Australia.

1b Choose a job
5– mins

- ↓ Write a few of the following jobs on pieces of paper and give them to students who can't decide on a job: pilot, teacher, doctor, singer, footballer, cook, taxi driver, fitness trainer, journalist

1c The instructions
5+ mins

- Students work in pairs and put the instructions in the right order and then check their answers in class.
left column: 1, 5, 2, 4; right column: 6, 3, 7

1d Play the game
15+ mins

Ask students to read through the questions on page 125 before playing the game *What's my job?*.
- ↓ Students can keep their books open at page 125 and refer to the questions.
- Demonstrate the activity by letting students ask you questions about 'your' job.
- Nominate an able student to lead the game and invite the class to ask him / her questions about the job he / she has chosen.
- If the class seems to be able to do this easily, have them guessing jobs in groups of five or six.

Part 2:
2a Meeting for a meal
1/53
5 mins

- ↓ Allocate one day of the week to each student.
- Students listen to a conversation to decide when Alun's students can meet. Play ▶ 1/53.

The only possible time they can meet is Thursday, for dinner.

(Al = Alun, B–D = three other students)
Al: OK, when shall we meet? How about lunch on Friday?
B: Sorry I can't on Friday, I work all day.
C: Yes, me too.
Al: OK ... well, how about another day ... for lunch?
B: The only days that are good for me are Saturdays and Sundays ... oh, and Wednesdays are good too, I don't work on Wednesdays.
Al: Oh dear, the restaurant isn't open at lunchtime at the weekends ... it never does lunches then ... only dinner in the evening. Well we could meet for lunch on Wednesday then.
C: No, sorry – not for me ... lunchtime is always a problem for me.
Al: So, let's say – "no lunch" ... right?
B + C together: Yep. That's right.
D: We could meet for dinner ... one evening?
Al: Yes ... Let's talk about the evenings. Shall we go out on Tuesday ...
Chorus of the others: No-o-o, No way ... that's our lesson!
Al: I know ... only joking.
B: Why don't we go out on Saturday or Sunday evening? We don't work then.
C: Oh ...sorry, I can't. I've got plans for next weekend.
D: Saturday *and* Sunday?
C: Yes, ... and Friday evening.
D: Hmmm – so now we have Monday, Wednesday or Thursday evening. Erm ... Monday?
Al: Not good for me – I play tennis every Monday evening.
B: And I stay at home with the children on Wednesdays ... my wife goes out.
D: So-o-o ... shall we go out on Thursday then?
Al/B/C: Yeah Thursday's good. / Great. / That's the best day.

2b How to say it
1/54
5+ mins

- Play ▶ 1/54.
- ↓ Allocate one phrase to each student.

Let's – 2, Why don't we – 1, We could – 2, How about – 2, Shall we – 3

2c Role play
10 mins

- Follow coursebook instructions.

2d Tell the class
5+ mins

- Follow coursebook instructions.

Part 3:
3a Six questions to ask
5+ mins

- ↓ Students can complete the questions in pairs.

Example questions: **1 meals / cups of tea, 2 meet friends, 3 go to bed, 4 start work, 5 What do you usually do in the mornings?, 6 have lunch**

If short of time

The **final activity** of the *Now I can* pages allows for time flexibility as it's often an open-ended activity. In ***Exercise 3b***, students can ask and answer questions in groups without having made notes about the answers.

3b And the answers?
10+ mins

- In groups, students ask each other their questions and chat about the topics.
- Monitor the activity, going from group to group, encouraging the more reluctant students.

And finally ...
5 mins

Point out the following features of the coursebook and give a short explanation:
- **Test yourself** (p. 42): Students can assess their progress by doing this test and checking their answers (p. 128).
- **Language and culture** (p. 43): Refer your students to any *L&C* texts and tasks that weren't read or done in class.
- **Now me** (p. 44): Students have the opportunity to personalise the structures they learnt in the previous unit and note down vocabulary which is particularly useful to them.

And point out ...
- the **Unit vocabulary** (p. 150–175), a chronological list of the words in the coursebook. Students can use it to practise the words they had in the unit – it's also useful if a student has missed a lesson and wants to catch up on the missed vocabulary. There are also lists of word groups and phrases from each step. The words can be listened to on the Internet – a code is provided (see the 'Tipp' on page 150).
- the **Dictionary** (p. 176–188), an alphabetical list of the words in the coursebook so students can easily look up unknown vocabulary from dialogues and exercises. These words can also be listened to on the Internet – a code is provided on page 176.

Does your course have more than the standard 24 lessons?
- After Units 2, 4 and 6, there is the optional section **Globetrotter**:
  Globetrotter Work – one page (45 minutes) of classroom material with the focus on English for work.
  Globetrotter Travel – one page (45 minutes) of classroom material with the focus on English for travel.
  A further 45 minutes of classroom material is provided on the Internet for each of these lessons.
  Teaching notes on **Globetrotter A** can also be found on pages 122/123.

Your notes

Unit 3 Step 1 A day in London

Contents

Storyline	Susan visits Mrs Benton, an old family friend.
Functions	Expressing interest
Vocabulary	Clothes
Grammar	**You already know:** Past simple – regular verbs **And now:** Past simple – irregular verbs

Lesson notes

Additional material

For optional and additional material for Unit 3, Step 1, see pages 85/86.
Refer to this section before your lesson as some of the materials require preparation.

Optional stages

Optional stages of the lesson are written in grey in these notes.

Photo page
5 mins

- Students look at the photos on page 47 and answer the questions.
  ! Point out the photo where Anna and Susan embrace as they greet each other. Remind students that it isn't customary in most English-speaking countries to shake hands when you greet friends – people say a casual *Hello* or embrace briefly.
- Refer students to *In dieser Unit lernen Sie u. a.:* ... and give them time to read about what they're going to learn in Unit 3.

Starter:
Your oldest relative
5– mins

! Relative = a person in your family
- Demonstrate the activity by telling the students about the oldest person in your family.

Tea with Mrs Benton
2/2
5+ mins

NB: This dialogue focusses on past events. Students who worked with *Network Now A1 Starter* are familiar with the concept of irregular verbs – *A1 Starter* introduced a limited number of them: *buy, come, do, go, have, meet, say, see, write.*
- Ask students to cover the dialogue. Refer them to the board and say: *Listen. What is correct?*
  Board:
  Mrs Benton shows Anna a photo of a) her children, b) her school, c) her wedding.
- Play ▶ 2/2.
- Play ▶ 2/2 again so that students can check the answer. (c) her wedding)

! There are some phrases which should be repeated as 'German interference' could be a problem: ... *a photo* ***of*** *my grandmother?* (not 'from'); *Your grandfather* ***took*** *it.* (not 'made'); ***When*** *I was eighteen* ... (not 'as').

Language and culture

The students can read the text *Getting married* (p. 63) and do the related tasks at home – or you can use this as a 'filler' if you have time at the end of the lesson. For more information on this, look at page 86 of this TRB.

1a Comprehension
5 mins

- Point out the ***Info box*** about the meaning of *suit.*
- Students can work individually or in pairs and cross out the wrong information.
  1 a suit / ~~a wedding dress~~, 2 ~~a handbag~~ / new shoes, 3 a blouse / ~~a hat~~, 4 ~~started~~ / stopped, 5 ~~in Leeds~~ / in London, 6 ~~emails~~ / letters

1b What did they do?
5+ mins

- Let your students decide for themselves how challenging they want this activity to be.
  Board:

*	Make two questions with: *wear / wedding dress; know / grandfather*
**	As in the coursebook.
***	Write four questions.

2 Grammar
5 mins

You already know: Past simple – regular verbs
! If some of your students are not very confident and want more revision practice, refer them to the *You already know* section of the *Language study* (p. 50). They can do the exercises in their book or online – tell them to go to www.langenscheidt.de/networknow/selfstudy and type in the Language study code which is given at the top of page 50. Online they find – in addition to the exercises from their book – extra practice of the *You already know* grammar from *Network Now A1 Starter*

And now: Past simple – irregular verbs
NB: Remind students that there is a list of irregular verbs on page 148 of their coursebook.

Read out the sentences in the *And now* grammar box and have the class repeat them in chorus.

2a What's the past form?
10– mins

- Give the class time to look through the text of the dialogue and underline the past forms.
- Check answers in class by nominating individuals to read out the sentence or phrase containing a past form.
  ! Here's an opportunity to nominate weaker members of the class as the activity is quite straight-forward.
  Your grandfather took it. I wore my best suit, ... I bought new shoes. Your grandmother gave me the blouse .... -she made it for me, ... a dressmaker before she got married, ... Yes, I knew him, ... Then she met your grandfather ... later they went to Canada. ..., we wrote letters every month and we sent photos .... I only saw your grandma when she came to England on holiday.

2b Ask and answer
5+ mins

NB: Look at the **Tip: Playing cards** (p. 85f.) for tips on getting students to work in pairs / groups.
- Demonstrate the activity by nominating a student and reading out the example exchange.
- ↓ Do the exercise as a class activity and, of necessary, do it twice.
- Students work in pairs and, in turns, ask each other the questions.
  1 Did Mrs Benton wear a wedding dress? – She didn't wear ..., she wore a suit. 2 Did she buy a handbag? – She didn't buy ..., she bought new shoes. 3 Did Jane make a jacket? – She didn't make ..., she made a blouse. 4 Did Mrs Benton get a job in ...? – She didn't get ..., she got a job in London. 5 Did Jane and Mrs Benton write emails? – They didn't write ..., they wrote letters.

3a Vocabulary: Clothes
10– mins

- Follow coursebook instructions

  4 blouse, 2 dress, 7 jacket, 1 pullover, 8 shirt, 5 skirt, 3 suit, 6 trousers

3b Choose your clothes
5+ mins

- While students are talking in pairs, monitor the activity and prompt reluctant students by asking them directly.
- Point out the ***Info box*** to remind students that *trousers, jeans, shorts* are plural (they have 2 legs!).

4a How to say it: Expressing interest
2/3–5
5+ mins

FYI: Diana Spencer married Prince Charles in St Paul's Cathedral on 29th July, 1981. They had two sons, William and Harry. Charles and Diana got divorced in 1996 – Diana died in a car crash in Paris in 1997.
- Play ▶ 2/3 and ask a volunteer to answer the question.

  They went to London because they wanted to see the royal wedding (Charles and Diana).
- Play ▶ 2/4 and students tick the phrases they hear.
  ✓ Oh really?, ✓ How interesting!, ✓ I didn't know that.

> (A = Anna, B = Mrs Benton)
> B: This is a photo of Jane and me in London. That was on Prince Charles and Diana's wedding day.
> A: Oh, really? I'm sure that was a wonderful day.
> B: Yes, it was. The city was full of people – thousands and thousands of people. Your grandmother was on holiday in England and she really wanted to see the wedding, so we went to London for the day.
> A: Did you see Charles or Diana?
> B: No, we didn't. There were too many people. But the atmosphere was fantastic and we really enjoyed the day.
> A: How interesting! My grandmother was in London for Charles and Diana's wedding day? I didn't know that!

- Finally, play ▶ 2/5 for students to listen and repeat the phrases in chorus.

1 Oh, really?	**2** Tell me more!	**3** How interesting!	**4** I didn't know that.

If short of time

If you notice you're getting short of time,
- do ***Exercise 4b*** as a class activity. Students can ask you about a visit you have made.
- do just one of the ***Round up*** activities.

4b Now you: A visit
5+ mins

- To make sure everyone has a specific visit in mind, ask students to write down *who* they visited, *when*, and *why*, before they start talking to a partner.

Round up
5a My day
10– mins

- Either hand out slips of paper or make sure students write on pieces of paper which can be collected.
- Follow coursebook instructions.

5b A party
5+ mins

- Demonstrate the activity by telling the class three or four sentences about a party that you went to.

Tip: Five-minute fillers One can never predict exactly how long a lesson is going to take – it depends on the size of the class, the ability of the students and the complexity of the language being focussed on. It's a good idea to keep a list of 'five-minute fillers' in case you have a few minutes left at the end of the lesson. There's space for this on page 189 of your coursebook. For some ideas, look at the **Tip: Playing cards, Use the cards for five-minute fillers** on page 86.

And finally ...
5+ mins

Remind students of the following:
- **Language study** (p. 50): Students can do this in their book or online – tell them to go to www.langenscheidt.de/networknow/selfstudy and type in the Language study code which is given at the top of page 50. Online they find – in addition to the exercises from their book – extra practice of the *You already know* grammar from *Network Now A1 Starter.*
- **Selfstudy** (p. 51): Students can do this in the book or online.
- **Keys** (p. 128) to the Language study and Selfstudy exercises.
- **Language and culture**, Step 1: *Getting married* and the corresponding tasks (p. 63). Encourage students to do the Internet task at home.

Unit 3 Step 2 Dinner with friends

Contents

Storyline	Anna goes to Susan and Tom's house for dinner and tells them about her visit to Mrs Benton.
Functions	Making compliments
Vocabulary	The weather
Pronunciation	[w] – *windy weather*
Grammar	**You already know:** Past time phrases (1) *(on Saturday, yesterday, last week)* **And now:** Past time phrases (2) *(a week ago, when I was young, When did you last ...?)*

Lesson notes

Additional material

For optional and additional material for Unit 3, Step 2, see pages 86/87.
Refer to this section before your lesson as some of the materials require preparation.

Optional stages

Optional stages of the lesson are written in grey in these notes.

Starter: Who is it?
5 mins

- Demonstrate the activity by describing someone in the class. Then invite students to do the same.

Dinner at Susan and Tom's house
2/9
5+ mins

- Ask students to cover the dialogue. Refer them to the board and say: *Listen. What is correct?*
  Board: Susan / Tom cooked dinner.
  Play ▶ 2/9.
- Play ▶ 2/9 again so that students can check their answer. (Tom)

Language and culture

The students can read the text *Gifts* (p. 63) and do the related tasks at home – or you can use this as a 'filler' if you have time at the end of the lesson. For more information on this, look at page 86 of this TRB.

1 Comprehension
10– mins

- Students tick the correct information and check their answers in class before correcting the false information.
  ✓ 3, 4; 1 ... ~~last year~~ five years ago, 2 ... a ~~history~~ cookery course, 5 ... ~~had~~ didn't have lunch, 6 ... ~~was~~ wasn't warm

2a Vocabulary: The weather
5+ mins

- Read out the sentences a) to f) and have students repeat them.
- Students match the sentences to the icons and check their answers in class.

1d), 2a), 3e), 4b), 5c), 6f)

2b Say it like this
2/10
5+ mins

- Students first listen to the pronunciation of *w*. Play ▶ 2/10.

! Many students find it difficult to produce the *w*-sound. First get the class to say *oo* (to rhyme with *who*). Then build up the words from that, so that they are saying: *ooweather, oowet*, etc.

- With a partner, students take turns to read the question and answer it.

2c How to say it: Talking about the weather
5+ mins

- Follow coursebook instructions.

2d A weather report
2/11
5+ mins

- First read out the place names on the map so that the students are familiar with them before they hear them on the CD.
  NB: The end of the word *Whitstable* is pronounced in the same way as the end of the word *vegetable*.
- ↓ Board: windy, sunny, wet, cloudy
  Tell the students to listen out for these words.
- Play ▶ 2/11. Students draw in the weather symbols.

- ↑ To check the answers, invite individuals to ask: *What's the weather like in (Whitstable)?* Give the place names as prompts.
  Whitstable – windy, Faversham – sunny, Canterbury – wet, Pean Hill – cloudy

> ... It's ten past six and time now to look at the local weather.
> There are strong winds from the North Sea today. People in Whitstable have a windy day in front of them!
> If you want sunshine, Faversham is the place to be – with temperatures of around 23° Celsius. Lovely and sunny – perfect for gardening or having an afternoon walk.
> But no afternoon walks in the Canterbury area – well, not without an umbrella! Rain, rain and more rain this afternoon and this evening. And a wet day tomorrow, too!
> Pean Hill is a bit better – no rain but a lot of cloud.
> So let's have some music to brighten our day – that old Simon and Garfunkel classic: *Cloudy ...*

3 Grammar
5+ mins

You already know: Past time phrases (1)
! If some of your students are not very confident and want more revision practice, refer them to the *You already know* section of the *Language study* (p. 54). They can do the exercises in their book or online – tell them to go to www.langenscheidt.de/networknow/selfstudy and type in the Language study code which is given at the top of page 54. Online they find – in addition to the exercises from their book – extra practice of the *You already know* grammar from *Network Now A1 Starter.*
- Ask individuals to make sentences with the phrases in the *You already know* box.
- ↑ Ask students to make questions with these phrases and to ask them to other students in the class.

And now: Past time phrases (2)
! There are some phrases which should be repeated as 'German interference' could be a problem: *a week* ***ago*** (not 'for a week'), ***when*** *he was in Italy* (not 'as').
- Have the class repeat the sentences in the *And now* section of the grammar box.

3a Time phrases
10+ mins

NB: Help your students to remember past time phrases by telling them this rhyme: *Yesterday, ago* and *last* always need the simple past.
- Have the students make a 3-column list with the headings from the blue box. Then they write the phrases under the correct heading.

last ...	... ago	when ...
– September – week – weekend – year	– four months – ten years – three weeks – two days	– he was a child – I started work – I was young – she was at school

- For the next part of the activity, students use the phrases they've written.
- Let your students decide for themselves how challenging they want this activity to be.
  Board:
  * Write sentences with these verbs: went, saw, phoned
  ** Write six sentences.
  *** Write three positive sentences and three negative sentences.
- Finally, each student reads out two of their sentences.

If short of time

If you notice you're getting short of time,
- do ***Exercise 3b*** as a class activity.
- do ***Exercise 5a*** as a class activity with students asking you questions.
- do just one of the ***Round up*** activities.

3b Now you: When did you last ...?
5+ mins

- Demonstrate the activity by asking an able student: *When did you last buy a newspaper?*
- Monitor the activity as students ask and answer questions in groups.

4a How to say it: Compliments
5+ mins

- Ask students to read out examples of compliments from the dialogue. *(This is very nice wine. What a lovely kitchen! That sauce smells wonderful.)*
  ! Remind the class of the difference between *this* (near to the speaker) and *that* (further away from the speaker).
- Do this as a class activity so that everyone hears plenty of examples of the structures.

4b Now you: That's a nice ...
5+ mins

- If students can't think of items, give prompt words: *bag – magazine – postcard – pullover – sandwich – book – chair*

Round up
5a About you
10 mins

- Demonstrate the activity by completing the sentences about you and letting students ask you questions.
- Then students do the same in groups.

5b Your favourite season
5– mins

- Follow coursebook instructions.

And finally ...
5+ mins

Remind students of the following:
- **Language study** (p. 54): Students can do this in their book or online – tell them to go to www.langenscheidt.de/networknow/selfstudy and type in the Language study code which is given at the top of page 54. Online they find – in addition to the exercises from their book – extra practice of the *You already know* grammar from *Network Now A1 Starter.*
- **Selfstudy** (p. 55): Students can do this in the book or online.
- **Keys** (p. 128 / 129) to the Language study and Selfstudy exercises.
- **Language and culture**, Step 2: *Gifts* and the corresponding tasks (p. 63).

And point out ...
- the **Lerntipp** on intonation at the end of the Selfstudy page (p. 55).

Tip: Personalisation (1) Students are more likely to want to speak about something if it directly concerns them – that's why there are *Now you* activities in the lesson and the *Now me* selfstudy pages where students can write about themselves. But the lessons can also be personalised if you and your students bring in relevant pieces of realia – cards, emails, photos, magazines, etc. At the end of this lesson, ask students to bring in greeting cards to the next lesson. (Never depend on students remembering to do this – it's just an added bonus if they do!)

Unit 3 Step 3 Special events

Contents

Realia	A wedding invitation
Functions	Invitations; Talking about life events
Vocabulary	Years
Reading	Greeting cards
Grammar	Imperatives *(Do that! / Don't do that!)*

Lesson notes

Additional material

For optional and additional material for Unit 3, Step 3, see page 87.
Refer to this section before your lesson as some of the materials require preparation.

Optional stages

Optional stages of the lesson are written in grey in these notes.

Starter:
My last invitation
5– mins

- If students have difficulty in thinking of an invitation, prompt them: an invitation to dinner, to a concert / a party / a wedding.

Invitations
1a A wedding invitation
10 mins

NB: Don't try to translate every word (e.g. *request the pleasure of the company of*) – the aim of confronting students with authentic materials is to encourage them to get the gist of texts.

- Students read the wedding invitation and then find the main information on it.
- Students ask the questions and nominate volunteers to answer.
  1 Her name's Lucy. 2 His name's Masters. 3 She's the bride's mother. 4 It's on Saturday, 22nd June. 5 It's at 2pm / two o'clock in the afternoon. 6 It takes place at St Mark's Church. 7 It's at The Hunting Lodge / Adlington Hall. 8 It means: *Please reply.*

Language and culture

The students can read the text *Invitations* (p. 63) and do the related tasks at home – or you can use this as a 'filler' if you have time at the end of the lesson. For more information on this, look at page 87 of this TRB.

1b Would you like to ...?
10– mins

- Have the class repeat some of the invitations in chorus.
- Then have them repeat the four sentences under the box.
- Point to one (able) student on your left and invite him / her to make an invitation.
- Point to a student on your right to respond.
- Do this a few times to demonstrate the activity, then students can work in pairs.
- Finally, individuals report to the class.

2 Grammar
5 mins

Imperatives: Do that! Don't do that!

- You're going to give instructions to the class. Demonstrate: *Touch your book*. Then ask the class to follow your instructions. *Touch your books. – Close your books. – Stand up. – Don't sit down. – Open your books. – Look at your partner. – Don't look at me. – Sit down. – Don't touch your books. – Look at me.*

2a Please be punctual!
5 mins

! Point out that imperative sentences can be softened by the word *Please*.

- Do the activity in class. Instruct the class: *Begin each sentence with 'Please'.*
- After the four examples have been done, ask for any additions.
  1 Please dance with me. 2 Please wear my favourite perfume. 3 Please be nice to my mother. 4 Please smile for the photographs.

2b Don't ...
5 mins

- Do the activity in class.
- After the four examples have been done, ask for any additions.
  1 Don't be late for the wedding. 2 Don't forget the rings. 3 Don't drink too much. 4 Don't wear your old shoes.

Special days

3a Reading: Greeting cards
10+ mins

Tip: Silent reading There are plenty of opportunities for students to read aloud – there's a dialogue in most steps. But the reading texts in Step 3 are designed for students to read them silently. Because the students don't read aloud, they are able to cope with cognates, like *billion, special, exam, Valentine,* etc. without worrying about the pronunciation. Being confronted with slightly more complex language shows them that they can understand a lot more written information than they think! Of course, once the students have read the text, you could then read it out to them, rather than have students read it aloud.

! The texts that students are presented with are getting gradually longer. We don't want to overwhelm the students, so split this text into three parts: Part 1, the questions; Part 2, the main body of the text; Part 3, *Did you know...?*

- Read out the three questions at the beginning of the text and ask individuals to answer them.
- Ask students to read the next part of the text silently and find the answers to the question on the board.
  Board: How much do people spend on cards in Britain? (£1.5 billion)
  NB: Billion is a 'false friend'. In German, a billion is 1.000.000.000.000 (12 zeros); in English, a billion is 1,000,000,000 (9 zeros).

Tip: Timing When you set a task in class, timing is often a problem. One group, or one student, is likely to finish before the rest of the class. So have a 'plus' task you can write on the board – an open-end task that students can busy themselves with until the others have completed the main task. Here, for example, students can highlight all the special days when people send cards.

- Students read the *Did you know ...?* part silently.
- Students will have read the text but may not know how to pronounce some of the words. Give several students the opportunity to repeat sentences from *Did you know ...?* by reading out a fact but making a deliberate mistake. The student must read out the correct sentence.
  1 *The average British person sends over <u>sixty</u>-five greeting cards a year.* (fifty-five)
  2 *<u>Men</u> buy eighty-five percent of the cards.* (Women)
  3 *At <u>Easter</u>, British charities ...* (At Christmas)
  4 *At Christmas, ... from sales of <u>Valentine's</u> cards.* (Christmas cards)
  5 *In <u>Germany</u>, many schools have ...* (In Britain)

3b Cards
5– mins

- Students (↓ in pairs) complete the sentences with words from the text.

1 wedding, 2 Valentine's, 3 Mother's, 4 Get well soon

- If you asked your class to bring greeting cards to the lesson, now is the time to look at them. Hold one up, ask what kind of card it is and who it was from.

An important year

4a Years
2/15
10– mins

- Point out the ***Info box*** about years and have students repeat the years in the box.
- Play ▶ 2/15 and have students repeat the years.
- Students read out the years around the class.

4b The first greeting card
2/16
5+ mins

FYI: Sir Henry Cole, the man who made the first commercial greeting card in 1843, was also the founder of the National Archives, which features in Unit 5.

- Give students time to read the text and tell them that two years are missing from the text.
- Play ▶ 2/16 so that students can write the missing years.

  1843, 2001
- Read out the three sentences, missing out the years and the price and invite individuals to insert the numbers.

> Well, greeting cards go back to Ancient China and Egypt. And in Europe there were greeting cards in the 1400s. But the first *mass produced*, *commercial* cards that you could send by post were the idea of Sir Henry Cole. He made the first commercial cards in 1843. And they were very popular – but they cost a lot of money. He sent a card to his grandmother and, do you know, in 2001, someone bought that card at an auction ... for £22,500! Sir Henry was an interesting man. He was the director of a museum. And later he started the National Archives where you can find out when people were born, when they got married, and when they died. Yes, an interesting man.

If short of time

If you notice you're getting short of time,
- ask students to complete just four sentences in ***Exercise 4c***.
- you write the year of an important personal event in ***Exercise 4d***, and the class can guess what it was.

4c Now you: Milestones in your life
5+ mins

- Tell students they must complete the sentences that are relevant to them.

4d Guessing game
10 mins

- Demonstrate the activity by writing a year that was important to you on the board and letting the class guess what your special event was.
- In turn, volunteers read out their years and the class guesses what the events were.

And finally ...
5– mins

Remind students of the following:
Language study (p. 58): An overview of the grammar of the step.
Selfstudy (p. 58): Students can do this in the book or online.
Keys (p. 129) to the Language study and Selfstudy exercises.
Language and culture, Step 3: *Invitations* and the corresponding tasks (p. 63).

And point out ...
Reading: The tatoo (p. 59): A a text 'just for fun' with a glossary of unknown words. For more information on this, look at pages 87 and 120 of this TRB.

Unit 3 Now I can

Contents

Review of vocabulary, functions and structures in Unit 3

Storyline	Alun and the other students talk about events in their past.
Starter	Making compliments; Clothes
Part 1	Talking about the past; Expressing interest; Talking about the weather; Years
Part 2	Invitations; Instructions
Part 3	Talking about the past; Talking about the weather

Lesson notes

Additional material

For optional and additional material for Unit 3, *Now I can*, see pages 87/88.
Refer to this section before your lesson as some of the materials require preparation.

Optional stages

Optional stages of the lesson are written in grey in these notes.

Jetzt kann ich u. a.: ...
5– mins

- Ask students to look at *Jetzt kann ich u. a.: ...* Remind them that the symbols refer to different skills or vocabulary items which they learnt in Unit 3 and were listed in the aims on the photo page (p. 47). Most of the tasks in *Now I can* focus on more than one skill or vocabulary item.

Starter:
The clothes in Unit 3
5+ mins

- If necessary, help students by pointing to different articles of clothing in the classroom and getting them to name the items.
- Before students start the compliments part of the activity, remind students that *shorts, jeans,* and *trousers* are plural by asking them to complete the sentences on the board.

Board:
Your shorts ________ nice.
________ his trousers blue or black?
Her jeans ________n't new.

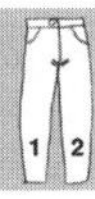

Part 1:
1a What was the event?
2/20–21
20 mins

- Tell students first to listen for information: *What was the event?* and *When was it?* and write it in the table. Play ▶ 2/20.

1 He ran in the London marathon, 1997. 2 His mother got married, 35 years ago. 3 He went to Disneyland (Paris) with his grandchildren, 2009.
Ask volunteers for the answers.

- Students then listen again, this time for details. They write them in the table.

↓ Write some key words on the board:
1 blind, slow
2 guests, picnic
3 Mickey Mouse, school holidays

Play ▶ 2/21.
e.g. 1 They ran to get money for a centre for blind people. They were slow – but not the slowest. 2 It was a small wedding – about twenty guests. The party after the wedding was a picnic. 3 He took a photo of his grandchildren with Mickey Mouse. It was very hot and there were a lot of people – it was the school holidays.

(Al = Alun))
1 Al: I always remember the first time that I ran in the London marathon – that was in 1997. I did it with a group of friends, six of us altogether. We did it to collect money for a day centre in our town – a day centre for blind people, especially for blind children after school and at weekends. One of the women in the group had a young blind daughter – and she often went to this day centre where they gave her extra help with her schoolwork. They did and still do now a wonderful job. We weren't so wonderful in the marathon. We were slow, very slow – *hours* behind the winners. But we weren't the slowest. The important thing was that we were there.

→

2 Al:	A day, from a long time ago, that I remember in every detail was the day my mother got married. I was 15 years old. So that's 35 years ago now. Goodness me – 35 years. It was a good day. She had a very small wedding – only about twenty guests. It's not everybody who can go to their mother's wedding, is it? This was her husband number two. Husband number one was my father – and I never saw my mother happy with him. I don't really know why. But with husband number two, she was always happy and she looked beautiful on her wedding day. She wore a nice dress – not a white wedding dress, I think it was blue. But the best thing was her party after the wedding. It was a picnic by the river – and she looked wonderful. That's how I like to remember her.
3 Al:	Another day that I remember was in 2008 ... no, it was 2009 ... I took my two grandchildren to Paris, to Disneyland. It was fantastic to see all the Disney characters there. Some were quite modern and others were really old – like Mickey Mouse, I can remember Mickey from when *I* was a boy. I think he's the most famous of all. I took a lovely photo of the two kids with Mickey. And I remember that it was very hot and that there were a lot of people because it was the school holidays. It was a special day too – there was a birthday party, I think, for one of the characters. They gave all the younger visitors a big ice-cream. It was a great day – for them ... and for me.

- Put students in groups of three and give them time to compare, and add to, the details they've written down.
- In their groups, each student presents one event to the group – or, if there's time, to the class.
- The groups vote on which event they would like to go to – a marathon, a wedding party, a trip to Disneyland – and tell the class.

1b Your event
10– mins

- Don't let students take too long in deciding on the event – if you notice a student hasn't started to write, offer him / her some suggestions: *Christmas, first day at school, a new flat, a carnival / Faschingsparty, their first English lesson, ...*

1c Other people's events
2/22
15+ mins

- Ask students to listen and make notes about the event.
- Remind students of the star system (see Unit 1, *Now I can*, p. 17) and write the options for doing the *Exercise 1c* on the board.
- Board:

  Make notes about the event:
  *   what it was
  **   where and when it was
  ***   details about the event

  Then in class, share the information.
  (* a concert by a Canadian singer; ** in Montreux, 2009; *** the concert was great, the concert hall was by a lake, it was a warm night)
- Play ▶ 2/22.

> I would like to tell you about a concert that I saw. It was a concert with Leonard Cohen. He's a Canadian singer. The concert was in Montreux, that's in the French part of Switzerland, in 2009. It was a fantastic concert. I first saw this singer in 1969 – such a long time ago. And I always liked him. I was always a big fan. So, I saw him in 1969 for the first time and then again 40 years later – yes, 40 years. And do you know – he was still good ... no, he was great ... even *better* than when he was younger. I went with a friend. She didn't know him before, but now she is a fan too. We went to Montreux on the train – a very nice trip there. And it was a wonderful evening. The concert hall was by the lake and the night was very warm.

- Ask students to go back to their groups of three with the notes they made about their special event.
- Point out the phrases in the speech bubbles on page 61, which can be used to express interest.
- Each student tells his / her group about their special event and the others express interest.
- Monitor the activity and express your interest – this will encourage students to do the same.

1d Top events in our class
10+ mins

- Ask students to vote for the most interesting event in their group and tell the class about it.

Part 2:
If short of time

If you notice, you're getting short of time,
- read out the informal phrases in ***Exercise 2a*** and have volunteers find the formal equivalent.
- let students from each group limit what they say in ***Exercise 3*** to three sentences – about the weather, the food and the people.

2a An invitation
10 mins

- ↓ Write the informal list on the board and, in class, students find the formal equivalent.
- Students work in pairs and write (F) or (I) next to the appropriate phrases.
  ! Students who finish very quickly can write out the formal invitation.

Informal	Formal
– Please come to our ...	– We would like to invite you to our ...
– Barbecue	– 6-course gourmet dinner
– In our back garden	– In Hadding Hall Hotel
– Bring a bottle	– Aperitif on the Lakeview Verandah
– Jeans, etc.	– Gentlemen: suits, please
– Come any time – after 6.	– Arrival time: 6 pm.
– Call us and tell us if you can come.	– RSVP

2b Do's and don'ts
5 mins

- Read out the examples in the speech bubbles on page 61, then follow coursebook instructions.
- If students can't think of advice, give prompts: (formal) eat before, punctual, jeans, formal clothes, reply; (informal) bottle of wine, formal clothes, before 6, telephone

Part 3:
What was it like?
5+ mins

- Encourage students to express interest and ask questions as the other group tells them about their event.

And finally ...
5 mins

Point out the following features of the coursebook and give a short explanation:
- **Test yourself** (p. 62): Students can assess their progress by doing this test and checking their answers (p. 129).
- **Language and culture** (p. 63): Refer your students to any *L&C* texts and tasks that weren't read or done in class.
- **Now me** (p. 64): Students can personalise their learning by writing short texts and noting down vocabulary which is particularly useful to them. Advise them to keep a record of their progress by assembling a dossier. Refer them to www.langenscheidt.de/networknow/portfolio.

Your notes

Unit 4 Step 1 In the gift shop

Contents

Storyline	Anna goes to the local gift shop to buy a wedding present for a friend.
Functions	Saying where places are in town
Vocabulary	Presents; Places in town
Grammar	**You already know:** *a / an* **And now:** *some / any*

Lesson notes

Additional material

For optional and additional material for Unit 4, Step 1, see pages 88/89.
Refer to this section before your lesson as some of the materials require preparation.

Optional stages

Optional stages of the lesson are written in grey in these notes.

Photo page
5 mins

- Students look at the photos on page 65 and answer the questions.
- Refer students to *In dieser Unit lernen Sie u. a.:* ... and give them time to read about what they're going to learn in Unit 4.

Starter: A great present
5– mins

- Demonstrate the activity by telling the students about the last present you bought – choose something simple that students know the word for, e.g. book, CD.

The gift shop
2/25
5+ mins

! Point out that the word *gift* means 'present' – it doesn't have the same meaning as the German word *Gift* (poison)!

- Focus first on the dialogue. Ask students to cover the dialogue. Refer students to the board and say: *Listen. What's correct?*
  Board:
  Anna buys a) an English teapot b) a bottle of champagne c) a vase.
- Play ▶ 2/25. (b) a bottle of champagne)
- Ask a volunteer for the answer and then play ▶ 2/25 again so that students can check the answer.

Language and culture

The students can read the text *Cash machines* (p. 81) and do the related tasks at home – or you can use this as a 'filler' if you have time at the end of the lesson. For more information on this, look at page 89 of this TRB.

1 Comprehension
5 mins

- Students answer the questions in class.

1 It's a gift shop. 2 She wants to buy a wedding present. 3 Because they have everything they need. 4 She needs some cash before she goes to the market. 5 It's in King Street, opposite the library.

2a Vocabulary: Presents
5+ mins

- Give the class time to read the list of gifts on the board outside the shop silently, then read out the list so that they hear the pronunciation of the words.
- Students then write the names of the gifts next to the pictures.
  1 vase, 2 biscuits, 3 jam, 4 teapot, 5 soap, 6 games

2b Now you: Think of a present
5+ mins

- Students work in pairs.
  Let your students decide for themselves how challenging they want this activity to be.
  Board:

*	My (best friend) would like ...
**	As in the coursebook.
***	Discuss suggestions for a present for your (best friend): What about ...? Does he / she like ...? You can give him / her ...

3 Grammar
5 mins

You already know: *a / an*
! If some of your students are not very confident and want more revision practice, refer them to the *You already know* section of the *Language study* (p. 68). They can do the exercises in their book or online – tell them to go to www.langenscheidt.de/networknow/selfstudy and type in the Language study code which is given at the top of page 68. Online they find – in addition to the exercises from their book – extra practice of the *You already know* grammar from *Network Now A1 Starter.*

And now: *some / any*
NB: In this step, students learn that *some* is used for positive statements and *any* for negative statements and questions. It isn't necessary to differentiate, at this stage, between countable and uncountable nouns – this comes in the Step 2.
- Read out the sentences in the *And now* grammar box and have the class repeat them in chorus.

3a In the gift shop
5 mins

They have some ... tea, coffee, jam, cakes, biscuits, toys, games, glasses, vases, teapots, soap.
- ↑ Ask for two items they have in a food shop, a pub, a fast food restaurant, a supermarket.

3b They have some ... but they don't have any ...
5+ mins

- Let your students decide for themselves how challenging they want this activity to be.
  Board:

*	First tick the items they have in the shop. Make sentences with *some*. Then, with the other words, make sentences with *any*.
**	As in the coursebook.
***	Do the coursebook activity. Then find more items on the board and make sentences with *some*.

They have some ... biscuits, coffee, soap, tea; They don't have any ... chocolates, coffee pots, wedding cards, whisky.

3c Now you: Do you have any ...?
5 mins

- Demonstrate the activity with an able student. Elicit the short answer: *Yes, I do* or *No, I don't,* not just one-word answers.

4a How to say it: Saying where things are in town
5+ mins

! Many students have a tendency to say: *It's opposite of / to the pub,* so give some examples to elicit: *It's opposite the ... – Where's the pub? Where's the library? Where's the school?*
- Choose weaker students to ask the question and they can nominate someone to answer.

It's in King Street. It's opposite the library. It's next to the post office / the office block. It's between the post office and the office block. It's near the school.

If short of time

If you notice you're getting short of time,
- do ***Exercise 4b*** as a class activity – have one half of the class look at page 123 and the other half look at page 124.
- do just one of the ***Round up*** activities.

4b Exchange information: Asking where things are in a town
10+ mins

Tip: Exchange information When doing a task where students do an A / B activity at the back of the book, clarity is the keyword. Put all the A students on one side of the room and all the B students on the other. Write *A:* and *B:* on the board and note down the page number. Ask each group to read their task together before pairing up with students from the other group.
- Follow coursebook instructions.

4c Where do they want to go?
2/26
5 + mins

- Say: *There are three dialogues. Listen. Where do the people want to go?*
  Play ▶ 2/26.

1 pub, 2 station, 3 Italian restaurant

1
A: Excuse me. Is there a pub near here?
B: Let me see. Yes, there's one in King Street, next to the library – you know, just opposite the post office.
A: Thanks very much.

2
C: Excuse me – where's the station?
D: It's at the end of Albert Road – near that big hotel. Look, you can see it from here – opposite the hospital.
C: Oh, right – thanks.
D: You're welcome.

3
E: Excuse me.
F: Yes?
E: Where exactly is the Italian restaurant – I know it's near here.
F: Yes, you're right. It's in King Street, next to the museum.
E: OK – thanks a lot.

Round up
5a Your town
5+ mins

- Have two students read out the example dialogue.
- Invite one student to ask you the first question and then shrug and say: *I'm sorry, I don't know* and write this on the board so that students have that option as an answer.
  Board:
  I'm sorry, I don't know.

5b Talk about it
10– mins

- The students are given the opportunity to talk freely about topics which have been covered in the lesson.

Tip: Correction (2) Increasingly, the students will be given opportunities to talk about subjects freely – without being given prompts, without having to use specific structures. Monitor these activities, giving assistance only if communication breaks down. The focus here is on communication, not accuracy. If students are constantly corrected while they're making conversation, this could inhibit them and they'll be reluctant to speak at all.

And finally ...
5+ mins

Remind students of the following:
- **Language study** (p. 68): Students can do this in their book or online – tell them to go to www.langenscheidt.de/networknow/selfstudy and type in the Language study code which is given at the top of page 68. Online they find – in addition to the exercises from their book – extra practice of the *You already know* grammar from *Network Now A1 Starter.*
- **Selfstudy** (p. 69): Students can do this in the book or online.
- **Keys** (p. 129) to the Language study and Selfstudy exercises.
- **Language and culture**, Step 1: *Cash machines* and the corresponding tasks (p. 81). Encourage students to do the Internet task at home.

And point out ...
- the **Lerntipp** on false friends at the end of the Selfstudy page (p. 69).

Unit 4 Step 2 At the farmers' market

Contents

Storyline	Anna and Susan go shopping at the local farmers' market.
Functions	Shopping phrases; Saying prices
Vocabulary	Food
Pronunciation	*of* [əv] – *a lot of eggs*
Grammar	**You already know:** *How much is it? / How much are they?* **And now:** *How much ...? / How many ...?* + countable and uncountable nouns

Lesson notes

Additional material

For optional and additional material for Unit 4, Step 2, see page 89.
Refer to this section before your lesson as some of the materials require preparation.

Optional stages

Optional stages of the lesson are written in grey in these notes.

Starter: Who is it?
5 mins

- Demonstrate the activity by saying where someone in the class is sitting and letting the class guess who it is. Then invite students to do the same.

How much would you like?
2/31
5+ mins

- Ask students to cover the dialogue. Refer students to the board and say: *What does Susan buy?*
  Board: bread – cheese – eggs
  Play ▶ 2/31.
- Play ▶ 2/31 again so that students can check their answer. (cheese, eggs)
- Point out the ***Info box*** about prices. Write these prices on the board and ask individual students to say them.
  Board: £3, £15, £11, £2, £30, £19

Language and culture

The students can read the text *Weights* (p. 81) and do the related task at home – or you can use this as a 'filler' if you have time at the end of the lesson. For more information on this, look at page 89 of this TRB.

1a Comprehension
5+ mins

- Give students time to complete the task and ask individual students to read out the answers.

1 are / ~~aren't~~, 2 ~~needs a lot of~~ / doesn't need much, 3 has some / ~~doesn't have any~~, 4 ~~needs a lot of~~ / doesn't need many, 5 ~~fifty-five pence~~ / five pounds fifty

1b Say it like this
2/32
5– mins

- Students practise the pronunciation of *a cup of* [əv] *tea.*
- Say: *Listen and repeat.* Play ▶ 2/32.

1 I'd like a piece of cheese.
2 I need a bottle of milk.
3 Could I have a kilo of apples?
4 I need a lot of eggs.
5 Can I have a box of chocolates?

1c Vocabulary: Food
5– mins

- Read out the items of food and have students repeat them.
- Students match the words to the pictures and individuals read out the answers.
  1 sugar, 2 rice, 3 onions, 4 potatoes, 5 oil, 6 meat, 7 bread rolls, 8 eggs

2 Grammar
10– mins

You already know: *How much is it? / How much are they?*
! If some of your students are not very confident and want more revision practice, refer them to the *You already know* section of the *Language study* (p. 72). They can do the exercises in their book or online – tell them to go to www.langenscheidt.de/networknow/selfstudy and type in the Language study code which is given at the top of page 72. Online they find – in addition to the exercises from their book – extra practice of the *You already know* grammar from *Network Now A1 Starter*.
- Give prompts and get students to ask the appropriate question: eggs – a teapot – cakes – onions – a bottle of champagne – a cup of coffee – bread rolls.

And now: *much, many, a lot of*
! Explain the concept of *countable* (you can count the items: 1, 2, 3, ...) and *uncountable* (you can't count the items).
- Say some items and ask the class to call out *Yes* if you can count them and *No* if you can't count them: *Can you count eggs? ... milk? ... wine? ... bottles of wine? ... biscuits? ... tea? ... cups of tea? ... sugar? ...cakes?*
- Have students repeat the sentences in the *And now* grammar box.

NB: Students can easily grasp the concept of *How much ...?* and *How many ...?* simply by equating the German phrases: *'Wie viel ...?'* and *'Wie viele ...?'*

2a *How much ...?* or *How many ...?*
5+ mins

- ↑ Students brainstorm the topic *Food and drink* and write the items on the board. Volunteers write (C) or (U) next to each item. They use these items, rather than the items in *Exercise 1c*, to do the activity.
- Follow coursebook instructions.
  Countable: **How many ... onions, potatoes, bread rolls, eggs would you like?**
  Uncountable: **How much ... sugar, rice, oil, meat would you like?**

2b Now you: Your eating habits
5+ mins

- Let your students decide for themselves how challenging they want this activity to be.
- Board: * Make questions with the food items in Exercise 1c.
  ** As in the coursebook.
  *** Use the verbs: *eat, drink, buy, cook.*

3a How to say it: Shopping
10– mins

- Tell the class that phrases a), b) and c) are phrases they could hear when they're shopping and have them repeat them after you.
- Tell the class that phrases d) – i) are phrases they could use when they're shopping and have them repeat them after you.
- Alone or in pairs students complete the sentences 1–3.
  1 f), h); 2 d), e), g); 3 i)

3b How to say it: Prices
5– mins

! Remind students that plurals are used for prices: £7.20 = seven pound<u>s</u> twenty.
- When students have filled in the missing words, they can ask the question to another student. This student chooses one of the printed answers.
  How much **is it**? How much **are they**?

3c At the market
2/33
5– mins

- Play ▶ 2/33 and students tick the prices they hear.

1c), 2b), 3c)
- After checking their answers, students read out the other prices.

1 Water melons. Lovely water melons. Water melons – two pounds twenty each or two for four pounds. Two twenty for one; four pounds for two.
2 Come and get your bananas – only ninety-six p a kilo. Bananas for ninety-six p ...
3 Bag of meat – lamb and beef. Thirteen twenty for a three kilo bag of meat. Just right for Sunday dinner – thirteen twenty and what do you get? A kilo of beef and leg of lamb a for ...

If short of time

If you notice you're getting short of time,
- do ***Exercise 3d*** as a class activity. Students make notes of the information required and then volunteer information to be written on the board.
- do just one of the ***Round up*** activities.

3d Fruit and vegetables
2/34–35
10+ mins

- Ask students to write down the items that Anna buys. Play ▶ 2/34.
- Ask students to listen again and write down the prices that Anna pays. Play ▶ 2/35.

½ kilo of tomatoes (£4.60 a kilo = **£2.30**)
4 kiwis (50p each = **£2.00**)
6 bananas (£1.50)
broccoli (42p)
4 oranges (40p each = **£1.60**)
Total: £7.82

(S = Stall holder, A = Anna)
S: Good morning. How can I help you?
A: Hello. Could I have half a kilo of tomatoes ... tomatoes, please. Er – how much are they?
S: These lovely tomatoes – they're £4.60 a kilo. And you want half a kilo?
A: Yes, that's right – just half a kilo. And those kiwis look nice – can I have four kiwis, please?
S: Yes – the kiwis are 50p each. It's a special offer this week – only 50p.
A: And I'd like some bananas, please.
S: Bananas – how many?
A: Er ... six, please.
S: Just a moment ... that's under a kilo ... that's one fifty-nine – but let's say £1.50.
A: Thank you. And I need some broccoli, please.
S: Broccoli – right – that's ... 42 pence. Would you like anything else?
A: One last thing ... I'd like four oranges, please – those over there.
S: Four oranges at 40 pence each. Is that all?
A: Yes, that's all, thanks.
S: OK. Now let's add all that up ...

Round up
4a The cost of living
5– mins

- Follow coursebook instructions.

4b Your partner
5– mins

- Demonstrate the activity by asking individual students a question from each of the three categories *(write, drink, have)*.

And finally ...
5+ mins

Remind students of the following:
- **Language study** (p. 72): Students can do this in their book or online – tell them to go to www.langenscheidt.de/networknow/selfstudy and type in the Language study code which is given at the top of page 72. Online they find – in addition to the exercises from their book – extra practice of the *You already know* grammar from *Network Now A1 Starter*.
- **Selfstudy** (p. 73): Students can do this in the book or online.
- **Keys** (p. 129) to the Language study and Selfstudy exercises.
- **Language and culture**, Step 2: *Weights* and the corresponding task (p. 81).

Unit 4 Step 3 Supermarket shopping

Contents

Realia A car park sign; Notices in shops
Functions Expressing permission and obligation
Vocabulary Shopping quantities
Reading Shopping online
Grammar **You already know:** *can / can't*
And now: *have to / don't have to*

Lesson notes

Additional material
For optional and additional material for Unit 4, Step 3, see page 90.
Refer to this section before your lesson as some of the materials require preparation.

Optional stages
Optional stages of the lesson are written in grey in these notes.

Starter: Car parks
5– mins
- Follow coursebook instructions.

The supermarket car park

1 Parking information
5 mins

NB: Bank holidays are public holidays and have existed since 1871. The name comes from the fact that banks were allowed to close on these days so no trading could take place.
- Students read the car park sign and tick the correct information.
  ✓ 1, 4

2 Grammar
5 mins

You already know: *can / can't*
! If some of your students are not very confident and want more revision, refer them to the *You already know section* of the Language study (p. 76). They can do it in their book or online – tell them to go to www.langenscheidt.de/networknow/selfstudy and type in the Language study code which is given at the top of page 76. Online they also find extra practice of the *You already know* grammar from *Network Now A1 Starter.*

And now: *have to / don't have to*
- Have the class repeat the sentences in both grammar boxes.
- Point out the ***Info box*** which tells them that 'you' is not only *Sie* and *Du*, but also *man*.
- ↑ Board:
  You can ... / You can't ...
  You have to ... / You don't have to ...
  Ask volunteers to make sentences with these phrases. *It's your first day at Kindergarten!*

2a Supermarket signs
5 mins
- In class, ask what the four signs mean.

1 You can go in the store here. 2 You can't take your dog into the shop. / Your dog has to stay outside. 3 You can buy two for seven pounds. / You don't have to pay £7.72 / full price. 4 You can't go in here.

2b Now you: Your English class
10+ mins
- Follow coursebook instructions.
- ↓ Elicit sentences by asking: *Can you smoke in the classroom / school? Do you have to speak English in the lesson / break? Do you have to do homework? Do you have to sit on the same seat every lesson? Can you speak German to the teacher? Do you have to pay for the course?* etc.

Possible answers: **You have to speak a lot of English; You don't have to speak English in the break; You can park near the school; You can't park in front of the school entrance.**

Buying things

3a At the supermarket
15– mins

NB: In AE, it's more common to use the word *can*, not *tin* for both drinks and food. In BE, *can* is usually used for drinks – *a can of cola*.

! Point to the photo of the jam and say: *This is a jar of jam. It isn't a glass – a glass is for drinking.*

- Students complete the phrases. Ask individuals to read out the answers: *Anna bought a ...* so the class can check their answers.
  1 shampoo, 2 biscuits, 3 potatoes, 4 jam, 5 soup
- Then students complete a shopping list with different items.
- **!** Because their vocabulary is still rather limited, encourage variations like: *mushroom soup / tomato soup, red wine / French wine*, etc.
- ↓ Before students write the shopping list, give them some ideas. Call out items and volunteers say the packaging and the item:
  (a jar of) *apple jam*, (a tin of) *tomato soup*, (a packet of) *tea*, (a bottle of) *Italian wine*, (a bag of) *apples*, (a packet of) *muesli*, (a bottle of) *whisky*, (a jar of) *instant coffee*.
  Possible answers: **A bottle of wine, A packet of cigarettes, A bag of apples, A jar of instant coffee, A tin of tomatoes**

If short of time

If you notice you're getting short of time,

- omit ***Exercise 3b***, the Shopping game.

3b Shopping game
5+ mins

- Students play the chain game where they memorise shopping items. Play the game only until it begins to get too repetitive.

Reading: Shopping online
10– mins

Tip: Key words Students have to be encouraged not to ask for the meaning of every unknown word in a text. When they have read the text silently, ask them to think about how much of it they could understand. If they couldn't understand the meaning of a sentence, which word prevented that? Invite individuals to ask the meaning of just *one word* from the text. Before they ask you, they should ask each other for help.

Board:

What does ____________ mean?

- Students read the text *Shopping online* silently and ask for any problematic vocabulary.
- To help them remember new words, use the 'repeat and complete' technique. Read out short parts of a sentence and have individuals repeat what you said and, from memory, add the missing last word, e.g.:
  You don't have to go to a (supermarket).
  You don't have to go to a supermarket to do your weekly (shopping).
  You can do it (online).
  In Britain, more and more supermarkets have (websites)
  and you can order your shopping (online),
  and the store delivers it to your (home).
  It's very (easy).
  First, you go to your supermarket's website and (register).
  You have to give your email (address).
  You have to give your email address and a (password).
  You have to give your name and address and your bank (details).
  Then you do your (shopping).
  You just click on the items that you want to (buy)
  and you choose a delivery (time).
  It's really (easy).
  They take the money from your bank (account)
  and deliver the items that you (ordered).

Language and culture

The students can read the text *Shopping online* (p. 81) and do the related task at home – or you can use this as a 'filler' if you have time at the end of the lesson. For more information on this, look at page 90 of this TRB.

4a Comprehension
5– mins

- Students first answer the questions in pairs, then individual students answer the questions in class.
  1 You have to give your email address and a password, your name and address and your bank details. 2 You have to click on the items you want to buy and choose a delivery time.

4b Pros and cons
2/40
10– mins

- Let your students decide for themselves how challenging they want this activity to be.
  Board:

*	Make notes about the positive <u>or</u> the negative aspects.
**	As in the coursebook.
***	Do ** and repeat to the class a sentence that you strongly agree with.

- Play ▶ 2/40.
  Positive: **It's easy and quick. You don't have to go to the supermarket after work. You don't have to carry heavy shopping.**
  Negative: **You always buy more. Maybe the food isn't fresh. You have to give bank details online so it's not safe.**

W: Dan – do you want anything from Cashshop? Wine maybe?
M: Oh, not Internet shopping again!
W: Come on, Dan ... it's so easy, and so quick – it means I don't have to go to the supermarket after work. You know I'm always tired after work and I don't want to go to the supermarket then.
M: Yes, but –
W: *And* I don't have to carry heavy shopping bags home.
M: Yes, and because you don't have to carry the shopping bags, you always buy more when you do the shopping online.
W: No, I don't. I buy the things we need.
M: And how do you know that the vegetables are fresh when you order them online? I like to see what I buy.
W: Of course they're fresh – it isn't any different from buying them in the shop – only that it's nice and easy.
M: And you know I don't like giving our bank details online – it's just not safe.
W: Dan, welcome to the twenty-first century! People do everything online – book holidays, tickets ... even find a partner.
M: Find a partner, eh? Hmmm ...
W: Dan!!!

4c Now you: What do you think?
10– mins

- While students are talking, monitor the activity, prompting only when communication breaks down. The focus is on communication not accuracy, and over-correction will inhibit rather than encourage communication.

And finally ...
5– mins

Remind students of the following:
- **Language study** (p. 76): Students can do this in their book or online – tell them to go to <u>www.langenscheidt.de/networknow/selfstudy</u> and type in the Language study code which is given at the top of page 76. Online they find – in addition to the exercises from their book – extra practice of the *You already know* grammar from *Network Now A1 Starter.*
- **Selfstudy** (p. 76): Students can do this in the book or online.
- **Keys** (p. 129 f.) to the Language study and Selfstudy exercises.
- **Language and culture,** Step 3: *Shopping online* and the corresponding task (p. 81). Encourage students to do the Internet task at home.

And point out ...
- **Reading: Markets around the world** (p. 77): A text 'just for fun' with a glossary of unknown words. For more information on this, look at pages 90 and 120 of this TRB.

Unit 4 Now I can

Contents — **Review of vocabulary, functions and structures in Unit 4**

Storyline Alun goes shopping.
Starter Food
Part 1 Asking what something costs and understanding prices; Shopping phrases; Shopping quantities
Part 2 Saying where things are in town
Part 3 Understanding signs and notices; Expressing permission and obligation

Lesson notes

Additional material For optional and additional material for Unit 4, *Now I can*, see pages 90/91.
Refer to this section before your lesson as some of the materials require preparation.

Optional stages Optional stages of the lesson are written in grey in these notes.

Jetzt kann ich u. a.: ...
5– mins

- Ask students to look at *Jetzt kann ich u. a.: ...* Remind them that the symbols refer to different skills or vocabulary items which they learnt in Unit 4 and were listed in the aims on the photo page (p. 65). Most of the tasks in *Now I can* focus on more than one skill or vocabulary item.

Starter:
The food in Unit 4
5+ mins

Tip: Pre-teaching vocabulary It's often comforting for the student to be presented with some of the new vocabulary before they try to do a task, read a text or listen to a dialogue. This doesn't mean that every new word should be introduced beforehand – pick out some key words which will make understanding the text easier, or give some items of vocabulary which your students will probably want to use actively, as in the *Starter* exercise below. But also encourage students to make use of the vocabulary they already know.

- Students may need a few new words for this exercise. Introduce them before the activity. Read out the sentences on the board so that the students hear the pronunciation of the new words. Ask individual students to read out the sentences, choosing the correct word (minced meat, bacon).
  Board:
  A hamburger is made of potatoes / minced meat.
  You need bacon / onions for an English breakfast.
- This can be done as a class activity, with students adding suggestions.
  e.g. Omelette – eggs, cheese, mushrooms, etc.; Spaghetti bolognese – pasta, onions, garlic, tomatoes, minced meat; Salami sandwich – salami, bread, salad; Lamb curry – meat / lamb, curry, rice; Fruit salad – apples, oranges, a melon, kiwis, etc.; Breakfast – eggs, bacon, mushrooms, coffee, orange juice, etc.

Part 1:
1a A trip to the supermarket
5+ mins

- Students work alone (↓ or in pairs) and put the events in chronological order.
  2, 7, 3, 8, 1, 9, 4, 5, 6
- Check answers by having individual students read out a sentence.

1b Alun's shopping trip
2/45
10– mins

- ↓ Make a list on the board of key words to listen for.
  Board:
  list – shop – bike – £
- Play ▶ 2/45.
  She made a list; Alan didn't make a list. He went to a small shop; she went to a supermarket. He went by bike; she drove. He paid cash; she paid by credit card.

(Al = Alun, P = Mrs Patel)
A: I went shopping yesterday – I always do my shopping on Fridays. I'm not really very good at shopping because I never make a list. I go to the shop, and I look around the shop and then I just buy the things I like! The problem is that I sometimes come home without the important things! Hhmm.
I go to a small shop in the centre of town – I always go on my bicycle. The lady who works there is very nice. She knows me and she knows what I like ...
P: Ah hello, how are you today?
A: Oh, I'm fine thanks ... and you?
P: Me too. How can I help you?
A: Erm ... oh yes, I need some bread and some cheese.
P: Here are your favourite bread rolls. How many would you like?
A: Erm ... three please ... no, four please. They *are* good.
P: And how much cheese would you like?
A: A small piece – about this big.
P: Ok, about 200 grams – yes?
A: Yes, that's fine. Erm ... and I need a jar of those small white onions – you know what I mean?
P: Yes ... these small white onions. Anything else?
A: Yes, I'd like a packet of tea – English breakfast tea please ... and oh yes, a packet of those wonderful chocolate biscuits that you always have!
M: English breakfast tea and chocolate biscuits. Is that all?
A: Yes, I think so ... Oh no, and a bag of apples, please.
P: A kilo?
A: Erm ... can I see? Oh, yes – that's fine.
P: Good. So that's £1.28 for the rolls, £1.60 for the cheese, £1.10 for the onions, £1.29 for the tea, £1.75 for the biscuits and £2.30 for the apples – that's £9.32 altogether.
A: £9.32 – so that's 5, 6, 7, 8, 9 pounds and 32 pence. Thank you!
P: Thank you – goodbye. See you next week.
A: And when I got home, I looked in the fridge and saw ... no butter, no milk! So I went back to the shop again in the afternoon. Typical me!

1c What did Alun buy?
2/46
20+ mins

- Let your students decide for themselves how challenging they want this activity to be.
  Board:
  * Write down the items.
  ** Write down the items and quantities.
  *** As in the coursebook.
- Play ▶ 2/46 and ask students to listen to Alun again.
- Check the answers in class and have students fill in any information they missed.
  4 bread rolls £1.28, 200 grams of cheese £1.60, a jar of (small white) onions £1.10, a packet of (English breakfast) tea £1.29, a packet of (chocolate) biscuits £1.75, a kilo of apples £2.30; Total: £9.32
- Refer the class to the words and phrases in the boxes on page 79 – these will help them to act out the dialogue.
- Students now work in pairs and act out the dialogue, adding one extra item to the shopping list.

Audio script: see above in *Exercise 1b*

1d Act it out
10 mins

- Two pairs of students work together and act out their dialogues.
- Follow coursebook instructions.

Part 2:
2a Make a quiz
10– mins

- ↓ Brainstorm 'buildings in town' and have two able students write a list on the board.
- Students work in pairs or small groups and write five sentences, using each of the words given.
- Monitor the activity, giving prompts where necessary.

2b Your quiz
10+ mins

- Demonstrate the activity. Say: *There's a bank near this school* and invite students to decide if it's true or false. If it's false, they should correct it: *There isn't a bank near here. There's a bank in (Ludwigstraße).*
- Students then read out their sentences to the class and the false ones are corrected.

If short of time

The **final activity** of the *Now I can* pages allows for time flexibility as it's often an open-ended activity. This one can be done as a class activity. A volunteer can draw a sign on the board and the class can guess what it means.

Part 3: Signs and their meanings
10– mins

- Ask students to look at page 126 and say what the signs mean.

  Possible answers: **You have to book a table. You can phone 378411 and book a table. – You can take your dog to this restaurant. Your dog doesn't have to stay at home. – You have to pay for your shopping before you leave the shop. You can't leave the shop before you pay. – Children can't go in here. – You don't have to buy a ticket. You can travel free. – You have to buy a ticket. You can / have to buy a ticket at the station. – You can't use your mobile phone. – You can't park here. You have to use the car park.**
- Students then draw signs or write three notices. Then, in groups, other students say what they mean.

And finally ...
5 mins

Point out the following features of the coursebook and give a short explanation:
- **Test yourself** (p. 80): Students can assess their progress by doing this test and checking their answers (p. 130).
- **Language and culture** (p. 81): Refer your students to any *L&C* texts and tasks that weren't read or done in class.
- **Now me** (p. 82): Students can personalise their learning by writing short texts and noting down vocabulary which is particularly useful to them. Advise them to keep a record of their progress by assembling a dossier. Refer them to www.langenscheidt.de/networknow/portfolio.

Does your course have more than the standard 24 lessons?
- After Unit 4, there is the optional section **Globetrotter**:
  Globetrotter B Work – one page (45 minutes) of classroom material with the focus on English for work.
  Globetrotter B Travel – one page (45 minutes) of classroom material with the focus on English for travel.
  A further 45 minutes of classroom material is provided on the Internet for this lesson.
  Teaching notes on **Globetrotter B** can also be found on pages 124/125.

Your notes

Unit 5 Step 1 Getting around

Contents

Storyline Anna phones Dave and asks for his help with her presentation.
Functions Telephoning; Comparing things
Vocabulary Transport
Grammar **You already know:** Adjectives *(fast, interesting)*
And now: Comparatives *(faster, more interesting)*

Lesson notes

Additional material
For optional and additional material for Unit 5, Step 1, see page 91.
Refer to this section before your lesson as some of the materials require preparation.

Optional stages
Optional stages of the lesson are written in grey in these notes.

Photo page
5 mins
- Students look at the photos on page 85 and answer the questions.
- Refer students to *In dieser Unit lernen Sie u. a.: ...* and give them time to read about what they're going to learn in Unit 5.

FYI: Kew is an attractive town on the Thames, south west of London. It's the home of the Royal Botanical Gardens (a World Heritage Site), the Royal Observatory, Kew Palace and The National Archives. There's an area of old shops, known as Kew Village, around Kew Gardens station.

Starter: Phone calls
5– mins
! Remind students that *to phone / to telephone* has no preposition following it:
I phoned my sister (**not** *to my sister* or *with my sister*).
- Demonstrate the activity by telling the students about the last phone call you made.

How can I help you?
3/2
5+ mins
- Board:
  Anna wants to speak to a) Susan b) Dave c) Tom.
- Refer students to the board and say: *Listen. What is correct?*
- Play ▶ 3/2.
- Ask a volunteer for the answer (b) Dave) and then play ▶ 3/2 again so that students can check the answer.

Language and culture
The students can read the text *The London underground* (p. 101) and do the related tasks at home – or you can use this as a 'filler' if you have time at the end of the lesson. For more information on this, look at page 91 of this TRB.

1a Comprehension
5 mins
- Students answer the questions in class.

1 It's next month. 2 She needs some old photos and maps of Faversham. 3 It's the National Archives. 4 It's bigger than the museum and their map archive is more extensive. 5 She can go by bus or by underground. 6 Yes, she can.

1b What did they say?
5+ mins
- Let your students decide for themselves how challenging they want this activity to be.
  Board:
  * Find one way to say each of these things.
  ** As in the coursebook.
  *** Do ** + one way to ask someone to wait + one way to make a suggestion.

1 Good morning, Hello, Hi; 2 My name's ..., This is ...; 3 Thank you, Thanks a lot;
(* One moment, please; Why don't you ...?)**
- When students have highlighted the phrases, ask volunteers to read out the sentence from the text.

1c Vocabulary: Transport
5+ mins

- Follow coursebook instructions.

1 car, 2 taxi, 3 bus, 4 underground, 5 bicycle / bike, 6 train

1d Now you: How do you go there?
5+ mins

NB: Although traditional usage is *by* car, bus, train, etc., and *on* foot, one hears more and more: *They went by foot* – even, sometimes, on the BBC!
- Point out the ***Info box*** and take a few minutes to explain the possible pitfalls.
  Board: I ~~drove~~ went by train, she cycled, and they went ~~by~~ on foot.

2a How to say it: Telephoning
10– mins

- Read out the first set of phrases and have the class repeat them.
- Do the same with the second set of phrases.
- Students then match the sentences with a similar meaning.
  1c), 2e), 3b), 4a), 5d)
- To check the answers, have one student read out a sentence from the first set and a volunteer to read the matching sentence from the second set.
- Ask which set is more formal (the first set).

2b A phone call
5+ mins

- Students read a short phone dialogue, first with formal phrases (printed) and then transfer it into an informal dialogue.
  A: Hello. What can I do for you?
  B: Hi, this is Anna (Turner). Can I speak to Dave (Evans), please?
  A: OK, just a minute.
  B: Thank you. / Thanks.

If short of time

If you notice you're getting short of time,
- omit the final activity in ***Exercise 2c*** – the writing and acting out the phone call.
- do ***Exercise 3b*** as a class activity.
- do just one of the ***Round up*** activities.

2c Anna's phone calls
3/3
10– mins

- Students listen to the beginning of four phone calls and choose the appropriate response.
- Play ▶ 3/3.

1a), 2b), 3a), 4b)

1	A:	Hello. Is that the National Archives?
2	A:	Hi Tom. Can I speak to Susan, please?
3	A:	Hello Mrs Benton. This is Anna.
4	T:	Sorry, Anna – Susan isn't here at the moment.

Tip: Roleplays If students are acting out phone calls, have the pairs of students sitting back to back so that they can't see each other's faces. And if you have students working in groups, give out roles occasionally – *Student A, you are Student B's teenage son; Student C, you're Student B's old neighbour.* Or you can sometimes vary the environment e.g. *you're in a car; you're in the dentist's waiting room; you're in a supermarket queue,* etc. This allows for the possibility of imaginative additions to the dialogues.

- Students then work with a partner, write a short phone dialogue and act it out in class.
- Let your students decide for themselves how challenging they want this activity to be.
  Board:

  Phone a partner and ...
  * tell each other what you did last weekend.
  ** tell each other what you did at work yesterday.
  *** invite him / her for dinner.

3 Grammar
5 mins

You already know: Adjectives *(fast, interesting)*
! If some of your students are not very confident and want more revision practice, refer them to the *You already know* section of the *Language study* (p. 88). They can do the exercises in their book or online – tell them to go to www.langenscheidt.de/networknow/selfstudy and type in the Language study code which is given at the top of page 88. Online they find – in addition to the exercises from their book – extra practice of the *You already know* grammar from *Network Now A1 Starter.*

And now: Comparatives *(faster, more interesting)*
- Read out the sentences in the *And now* grammar box and have the class repeat them in chorus.

3a Now you: Comparisons
5 mins

- As this is a fairly simple exercise, choose weaker student to read out their sentences.

3b Town and city
5 mins

- Put the class in groups, then demonstrate the activity with an able student.

Round up
4a Famous people chain
5+ mins

- First brainstorm famous people – the people must be alive. Call out the following categories and have students call out two or three names: *A sports person? A film star? A TV personality? A singer? A politician? A famous American? A famous British person?*
- Then demonstrate the chain game before students play it in class.

4b Talk about it
5+ mins

- This activity can be done in pairs or in class.
- If you have time left, you can do a similar activity with favourite restaurant and favourite shop.

And finally ...
5+ mins

Remind students of the following:
- **Language study** (p. 88): Students can do this in their book or online – tell them to go to www.langenscheidt.de/networknow/selfstudy and type in the Language study code which is given at the top of page 88. Online they find – in addition to the exercises from their book – extra practice of the *You already know* grammar from *Network Now A1 Starter.*
- **Selfstudy** (p. 89): Students can do this in the book or online.
- **Keys** (p. 130) to the Language study and Selfstudy exercises.
- **Language and culture,** Step 1: *The London underground* and the corresponding tasks (p. 101). Encourage students to do the Internet task at home.

Unit 5 Step 2 Asking for directions

Contents

Storyline	Anna asks for directions to the National Archives.
Functions	Giving directions
Vocabulary	In the street
Pronunciation	*It's one of the best …* (running words together)
Grammar	**You already know:** Comparatives *(faster, more interesting)* (see Unit 5 Step 1) **And now:** Superlatives *(the fastest, the most interesting)*

Lesson notes

Additional material
For optional and additional material for Unit 5, Step 2, see pages 91/92.
Refer to this section before your lesson as some of the materials require preparation.

Optional stages
Optional stages of the lesson are written in grey in these notes.

Starter: Comparisons
5 mins
- Demonstrate the activity by making two or three sentences comparing, for example, the town you're in with your home town / you and someone in your family / the classroom and your living room. Then invite students to do the same.

Can you tell me the way, please?
3/7
5+ mins
- Ask students to cover the dialogue. Refer students to the map and say: *Highlight the names of the roads that you hear.* Play ▶ 3/7.
- Play ▶ 3/7 again so that students can check their answer. (Burlington Avenue, Mortlake Road)

Language and culture
The students can read the text *Roads and streets* (p. 101) and do the related task at home – or you can use this as a 'filler' if you have time at the end of the lesson. For more information on this, look at page 92 of this TRB.

1a Comprehension
5 mins
NB Pronunciation: With roads, avenues, gardens, terraces, etc., the stress is *not* on the name: Mortlake Road, Kew Gardens, Ruskin Avenue. (With streets, the stress *is* on the name: King Street, High Street.)
- Students do the exercise alone and then compare answers in class by reading out the correct sentences.
  1 ~~by bus~~ / by underground, 2 directions / ~~the time~~, 3 has to / ~~doesn't have to~~, 4 ~~aren't many~~ / are a lot of, 5 busiest / ~~quietest~~, 6 his business card / ~~a postcard~~

1b Vocabulary: In the street
5– mins
- Read out the six vocabulary items and have the class repeat them in chorus.
- Give students time to do the exercise alone, then ask individuals for the answers: *(Klaus), what's number one?*
  ! Point out that *traffic lights* are always plural: *The traffic lights are green.*
  1f), 2a), 3e), 4c), 5d), 6b)

2a How to say it: Asking for directions
5+ mins
- Students match the sentence halves and read out the correct answers.

  1b), 2a), 3c)
- Practise the phrases by giving prompt words and asking individual students to put the word into one of the phrases: *bus stop, bank, post office, tube station, supermarket, post box, hospital, pub, restaurant*
  ↓ Board:

  Where's the nearest ______________, please?
  Could you tell me the way to the ______________, please?
  Excuse me, is there a ______________ near here?

2b How to say it: Giving directions

3/8+10

10– mins

- Students listen and tick the phrases they hear. Play ▶ 3/8.

✓ 2, 4, 7

(M = man, W = woman) W: ... Yes, that's right. Do you know it? M: Oh yes – and it isn't too far. Go along Station Avenue. Take the first street on your right. Go past the bank. And it's on the left – before you get to the main road. W: Station Avenue and then first right. OK – thanks very much. M: You're welcome.

- Students then listen and repeat the seven phrases. Play ▶ 3/10.

2c Where is it?

3/9

5– mins

- Students listen again to the woman (see above) and mark her route on the map on page 90 to find out where she wants to go. Play ▶ 3/9.

6 – the Catholic church

2d It isn't far

10– mins

Demonstrate the activity in class. Go from the station to the bus stop (2). Ask volunteers to give just one direction.

- Students work in pairs and take turns in giving directions.
  Let your students decide for themselves how challenging they want this activity to be.
  Board:
  * Your partner asks you for directions to a place on the map.
  ** As in the coursebook.
  *** Don't take the most direct route.

3 Grammar

10– mins

You already know: Comparatives *(faster, more interesting)*

- Ask a student to read the first sentence. Then ask another student to make a similar sentence with: *slower / dirtier*. Do the same with the second sentence and give the substitution words: *pretty / nice*. And for the third sentence: *expensive / comfortable*.
- Remind the class that to make the comparative of short adjectives, we add *er (smaller)*; to make the comparative of long adjectives, we add *more (more expensive)*.

! If some of your students are not very confident and want more revision practice, refer them to the *You already know* section of the *Language study* (p. 92). They can do the exercises in their book or online – tell them to go to www.langenscheidt.de/networknow/selfstudy and type in the Language study code which is given at the top of page 92. Online they find – in addition to the exercises from their book – extra practice of the *You already know* grammar from *Network Now A1 Starter*.

And now: Superlatives *(the fastest, the most interesting)*

NB Pronunciation: Palm House – *palm* rhymes with *arm* – the *L* is silent.

- Ask a student to read the first sentence. Then ask another student to make a similar sentence with: *slowest / nicest*. Do the same with the second sentence and give the substitution words: *dirty / friendly*. And for the third sentence: *exciting / beautiful*.
- Tell the class that to make the superlative of short adjectives, we add *est (smallest)*; to make the superlative of long adjectives, we add *most (most expensive)*.

3a It's one of the ...

10– mins

- Point out the photo of platform 9 ¾ and ask if anyone knows where that is.
  FYI: King's Cross Station
  Next to King's Cross railway station is St Pancras station, and they share one underground station: King's Cross St Pancras. King's Cross is famous for being featured in J K Rowling's *Harry Potter* books. Platform 9 ¾, reached by passing through a wall between platforms 9 and 10, is the starting point of the Hogwarts Express.

- **!** Remind students of the spelling rules in the Language study on page 88 (biggest, busiest). Students work alone (↓ or in pairs) and complete the sentences.
- Answers can be checked by doing *Exercise 3b*.
  1 the oldest, 2 the biggest, 3 the busiest, 4 the most attractive, 5 the most interesting

3b Say it like this
3/11
5– mins

- Play ▶ 3/11 and have students check their answers in *Exercise 3a* and repeat the phrases.

1	one of the oldest London Bridge is one of the oldest stations.
2	one of the biggest Waterloo is one of the biggest stations.
3	one of the busiest Victoria is one of the busiest stations.
4	one of the most attractive Kew is one of the most attractive stations.
5	one of the most interesting King's Cross is one of the most interesting stations.

If short of time

If you notice you're getting short of time,
- ask students to choose just one of the options in each question in ***Exercise 3b***.
- do just one of the ***Round up*** activities.

Round up
4a Your favourite restaurant
5– mins

- Follow coursebook instructions.

4b Talk about it
5– mins

- This can be done as a class activity. Join in with the exercise to encourage students to express different opinions: *Really? Well, I think (Paris) is dirtier than London.*

And finally ...
5+ mins

Remind students of the following:
- **Language study** (p. 92): Students can do this in their book or online – tell them to go to www.langenscheidt.de/networknow/selfstudy and type in the Language study code which is given at the top of page 92. Online they find – in addition to the exercises from their book – extra practice of the *You already know* grammar from *Network Now A1 Starter*.
- **Selfstudy** (p. 93): Students can do this in the book or online.
- **Keys** (p. 130) to the Language study and Selfstudy exercises.
- **Language and culture,** Step 2: *Roads and streets* and the corresponding task (p. 101).

And point out ...
- the **Lerntipp** on Learning words and structures at the end of the Selfstudy page (p. 93). Remind students that there is a Unit Vocabulary section (pages 150–175) to help them learn vocabulary. Also mention that there is a section of Lerntipps on pages 190/191.

Unit 5 Step 3 Travelling by bus

Contents

Realia	A bus timetable
Functions	Asking for bus information
Vocabulary	Numbers
Pronunciation	Stress in questions
Reading	England by bus
Grammar	**You already know:** *cheap, cheaper, the cheapest* (see Unit 5 Step 1 + Step 2) **And now:** *good, better, the best / bad, worse, the worst*

Lesson notes

Additional material

For optional and additional material for Unit 5, Step 3, see pages 92/93.
Refer to this section before your lesson as some of the materials require preparation.

Optional stages

Optional stages of the lesson are written in grey in these notes.

Starter: Tickets
5– mins

Tip: Realia If you take realia into the lesson, it adds to the authenticity of the task. Here, for example, you could have a variety of tickets you could hand out to pairs of students and ask them to say what kind of tickets they are and find any other information on them. Keep a box of labelled envelopes containing realia for *Network Now A1*, e.g. **Unit 5 Step 3: Tickets.** You can also organise the photocopiable materials in this book (pages 98 – 118) in the same way. This will make your lesson planning much quicker the next time you teach this course.

- Be ready to demonstrate the activity with a ticket of your own.

The bus timetable
1a What's right?
5+ mins

- Give students time to understand the layout of the timetable and then, alone (↓ or in pairs), they can tick the correct information.
  ✓ 1, 5
- ↑ Students can correct the false information by making negative sentences. Say: *Correct the false sentences. Use 'doesn't' or 'don't'.* (2 This bus doesn't go to Richmond. 3 The buses don't run all night. 4 The journey doesn't take more than thirty minutes.)
- ↑ In pairs, students write a similar true / false sentence based on the timetable, and exchange sentences with another pair.

1b Asking for information
3/16
10– mins

- Give students time to read through the questions and then play ▶ 3/16.
- **!** They'll probably need to hear the recording twice.

5, 4, 2, 1, 3
- Check the answers and have the class repeat the questions in chorus.

1 No, I don't have a free bus pass, young man. I'm only 59 so I have to pay!
2 Oh dear, all that shopping. Let's go back to the hotel now and have some coffee. Where's my bus timetable? Here it is. Let's see ... what's the time now? It's twenty past two – so how long do we have to wait ...?
3 Well, the party is from 8 o'clock so I think we have to come home on the all-night train. Or maybe there's a bus after midnight. A bus would be better – but how late do they run? Let's look online ...
4 Oh dear – is this the bus to Kew or ... or Hammersmith? Excuse me – am I on the right bus?
5 Excuse me, can you help me, please. I want to go to Richmond – I need the 391 bus.

1c Information
10– mins

- Students match the questions to the answers.
- Check the answers in class before students read the mini-dialogues in pairs.
  2a), 5b), 1c), 4d), 3e)

Travelling around
2a Logic puzzle
10 mins

- Start the activity off by reading through the information and getting students to write in the information about Jenny. (She went by bus; the journey cost nothing.)
- Ask students to work in pairs and direct them to sentence three, the one about Oliver.
  Jenny – bus – Sands End – nothing;
  Peter – taxi – Richmond – £25;
  Oliver – train – Hammersmith – £32;
  Fred – bike – Kew – nothing

Language and culture

The students can read the text *Double-decker buses* (p. 101) and do the related task at home – or you can use this as a 'filler' if you have time at the end of the lesson. For more information on this, look at page 93 of this TRB.

2b Now you: Your journey
5+ mins

- Follow coursebook instructions.

Reading: England by bus
10– mins

- Students read *England by bus* silently and ask for any problematic vocabulary which hampers their understanding.
  ! Point out the difference in titles: *Miss Clarke* and *Mrs Taylor*. Ask what that tells us about the women. (*Miss* Clarke isn't married; *Mrs* Taylor is, or was, married.) Ask what the more modern title is, which we can use for married *or* unmarried women. (Ms)
- Ask a few questions to check comprehension: *Can all people travel free on English buses?* (No – only people over sixty.) *How long was Sally and Fran's journey*? (Eight days.) *What did they collect money for?* (Their church.) *What was the low point of their journey?* (They got lost.) *And the high point?* (Fran's seventy-second birthday.)

! Point out the ***Info box*** about numbers before students do *Exercise 3a*.

3a Remember the text: Numbers
5+ mins

- Follow coursebook instructions.
- ↓ Students can refer to the text when they do the exercise.

  Example sentences: **1 People over sixty can travel free on buses after <u>half past nine</u> in the morning. 2 Sally Clarke is <u>sixty-eight</u> and Fran Taylor is <u>seventy-two</u>. 3 It was an <u>eight</u>-day journey. 4 They travelled <u>eight hundred and eighty</u> kilometres. 5 They travelled on <u>thirty-three</u> different buses. 6 It didn't cost <u>one</u> penny. 7 They got <u>three thousand</u> pounds for their local church. 8 Mrs Taylor celebrated her <u>seventy-second</u> birthday outside Exeter Cathedral.**

If short of time

If you notice you're getting short of time,
- limit the number of details you ask for in ***Exercise 3b***, question 3.

3b In your own words
10– mins

- If you have time, you can ask students to write their answers and then have individuals read them out to the class. If you do this, allow 10 minutes for the exercise.
- ↓ Give prompts for question 3:
- north to south – eight days – cost – places – sponsored – lost – birthday
  Example sentences:
  1 **Because in England, people over sixty can travel free on buses and Fran is 72 and Sally is 68.**
  2 **People sponsored their journey because ... they thought the journey was fun / they wanted to help Fran's local church.**
  3 **The journey was from the north of England to the south. It took eight days. It cost nothing. They saw interesting places. People sponsored their journey. They got lost. Fran celebrated her seventy-second birthday outside Exeter Cathedral.**

4 Grammar
5 mins

You already know: *cheap, cheaper, the cheapest*
! If some of your students are not very confident and want more revision, refer them to the *You already know section* of the Language study (p. 96). They can do it in their book or online – tell them to go to www.langenscheidt.de/networknow/selfstudy and type in the Language study code which is given at the top of page 96. Online they also find extra practice of the *You already know* grammar from *Network Now A1 Starter.*

And now: *good, better, the best / bad, worse, the worst*
- Have the class repeat the sentences in both grammar boxes.

4a Complete the sentences
5 mins

Students write in the correct words and then read one of the short texts to a partner.

1 (a) good, (b) better, (c) best;
2 (a) worst, (b) bad, (c) worse

4b Now you: Your journeys
5 mins

- Demonstrate the activity by telling the class three or four things about your best or worst journey.
- ↓ Board:
  Where did you go? And why?
  When did you go?
  How did you travel?
  Who did you go with?
  Why was it your best / worst journey?

And finally ...
5– mins

Remind students of the following:
- **Language study** (p. 96): Students can do this in their book or online – tell them to go to www.langenscheidt.de/networknow/selfstudy and type in the Language study code which is given at the top of page 96. Online they find – in addition to the exercises from their book – extra practice of the *You already know* grammar from *Network Now A1 Starter.*
- **Selfstudy** (p. 96): Students can do this in the book or online.
- **Keys** (p. 130) to the Language study and Selfstudy exercises.
- **Language and culture,** Step 3: *Double-decker buses* (p. 101). Encourage students to do the Internet task at home.

And point out ...
- **Reading: Taxi!** (p. 97): Two texts 'just for fun' with a glossary of unknown words. For more information on this, look at pages 93 and 120/121 of this TRB.

Unit 5 Now I can

Contents

Review of vocabulary, functions and structures in Unit 5

Storyline	Alun has a visitor from Germany.
Starter	Big numbers
Part 1	Comparing things; Asking the way and giving directions; Getting local travel information
Part 2	Asking the way and giving directions
Part 3	Making phone calls

Lesson notes

Additional material

For optional and additional material for Unit 5, *Now I can*, see pages 93/94.
Refer to this section before your lesson as some of the materials require preparation.

Optional stages

Optional stages of the lesson are written in grey in these notes.

Jetzt kann ich u. a.: ...
5– mins

- Ask students to look at *Jetzt kann ich u. a.: ...* Remind them that the symbols refer to different skills or vocabulary items which they learnt in Unit 5 and were listed in the aims on the photo page (p. 85). Most of the tasks in *Now I can* focus on more than one skill or vocabulary item.

Starter:
The numbers in Unit 5
10– mins

- Write the numbers on the board so students can refer to them as they say the numbers.

five ››› fifty-five ››› five hundred and fifty-five ››› five thousand, five hundred and fifty-five ››› fifty-five thousand, five hundred and fifty-five ››› five hundred and fifty-five thousand, five hundred and fifty-five ››› five million, five hundred and fifty-five thousand, five hundred and fifty-five
Numbers under the photos: **three ››› forty-four ››› five hundred and fifty-five ››› six thousand, six hundred and sixty-six ››› seventy-seven thousand, seven hundred and seventy-seven ››› eight hundred and eighty-eight thousand, eight hundred and eighty-eight ››› nine million, nine hundred and ninety-nine thousand, nine hundred and ninety-nine**
- When students make sentences with the big numbers, they may need prompts: *pubs, tourists, people, schools, shops*

Part 1:
1a The information hotline
3/20
10 mins

- Read out the instructions and then play ▶ 3/20 – twice if necessary.
- ↓ Board:

1 ____________ suggestions for places to stay in ____________ in ____________.
2 Public ____________. Special tickets for ____________.
3 How to go from ____________ to ____________.

- Have students compare their answer in class.

1 **3 suggestions for places to stay in the town centre (hotel or bed & breakfast) in September. Size / Cost / Location.**
2 **Public transport – trains, buses, trams. Special tickets for visitors and older people?**
3 **How to go from the station to the hospital. Can only walk 1 km.**

1 Hello – hello – oh ... my message ... yes, ok – I want to visit some friends in September but I don't want to stay with them. I want to stay in a hotel or a bed and breakfast in the centre. Can you please give me some information on three places perhaps? Can you compare them for me – how big they are, how expensive and, of course, the location? Nice places, please! Thanks very much. Goodbye. Oh, my phone number is ...
2 Hello – I would like some information about public transport in your area. I want to come and live there and I don't have, and don't want to have, a car. I'd like to know about trains, buses, trams, etc. in the area. Oh and I always have a lot of visitors – so is there some kind of visitor's ticket for a day or for two or three days? Or are there any special tickets for older people? Thanks a lot. You can call me on ...

→

> 3 Hello – one of my friends is in the hospital, and I want to visit him. Can you please tell me how to get from the station to the hospital? I can walk about a kilometre but not more than that ... I'm 79, you know. Can you help me with this? I'm at home every morning ... my telephone number is ...

1b Helpful answers
10– mins

- Students work in groups of three and prepare answers to the questions in *Exercise 1a*, relating them to their town.

1c The same answers?
10 mins

- Students compare answers in class. Ask volunteers the questions: *Where can a visitor stay in this town? What do you know about the exact location / the type of room / the cost? What can you say about the public transport in this town? What kind of tickets can you buy? How can you travel from the main station to the hospital?*

Part 2:
If short of time

Use the suggested simple version of ***Exercise 2a*** and the simple version of ***Part 3***.

2a Alun's visitor from Germany
10+ mins

- Read out the mail slowly and check that the meaning is clear.
- Make copies of the map on page 93 and offer the copies to the students. Get them to read Alun's mail again and label the buildings on the map.
  A: Chinese takeaway, B: cinema, C: Alun's house, D: bank, E: Italian restaurant, F: station

Tip: Photocopies If you want to photocopy an activity which is smaller than A4, copy the item several times and stick the copies onto one piece of paper. Then you simply have to copy that one piece of paper a couple of times to have a set of copies for the class. And make a file of these papers (with the unit number and step number written on them) and this will really speed up your lesson preparation.

2b A good map?
5 mins

- Students compare the map they've drawn (↓ or completed) and rate their map.

2c Your town
10 mins

- Follow coursebook instructions.
  ! If your students don't all live locally, let the students read their directions to the class so that more people will be involved in guessing the destination.
- ↓ Write directions from the school to the nearest bus / tram stop or train / tube station and compare with a partner.

Part 3:
A phone call to Alun's hotel
3/21
15+ mins

- Remind the class that Alun works in a hotel. He's on the phone at the reception desk. Ask: *Does the caller want to speak to Alun?*
- Play ▶ 3/21 and ask for the answer. (No, he doesn't.)
- Refer students to page 126 and play ▶ 3/21 again.
- Give students time to fill in the missing parts of the dialogue on page 126.
- ↓ Make copies of the responses on page 94 – one for each student. In pairs, students find the correct responses and then write them in the grid on page 126 in their coursebook.
  D, F, C, B, A, G, E
- Play ▶ 3/21 again so they can check that their answers fit in with the dialogue.
- Students act out the dialogue in pairs.

(Al = Alun) Al: The Linden Hotel, good morning. … Al: Yes, this is the reception. What can I do for you? … Al: I'm sorry, she isn't here today. Would you like to phone later? … Al: Yes, of course you can ask me a question … … Al: And what's your question? … Al: Yes, come out of the station. Turn left and walk about 200 metres. The hotel is on your left. … Al: You're welcome. Goodbye. …	**Good morning. Is that the reception?** **Can I speak to (Petra), please?** **Er, no, it's OK – but can I ask you a question?** **Thank you.** **Could you tell me the way from the station to your hotel, please?** **Oh good, I can walk there. Thanks very much.** **Bye.**

And finally …
5 mins

Remind students of the following:

- **Test yourself** (p. 100): Students can assess their progress by doing this test and checking their answers (p. 130).
- **Language and culture** (p. 101): Refer your students to any *L&C* texts and tasks that weren't read or done in class.
- **Now me** (p. 102): Students can personalise their learning by writing short texts and noting down vocabulary which is particularly useful to them. Advise them to keep a record of their progress by assembling a dossier. Refer them to www.langenscheidt.de/networknow/portfolio.

Your notes

Unit 6 Step 1 Anna's presentation

Contents

Storyline Anna writes an email to Dave, telling him what she's going to do in her presentation.

Functions Talking about future plans; Preparing a presentation; Structuring ideas

Vocabulary Putting information in order *(First …; Next …)*

Pronunciation *going to* [tə] *do*

Grammar **You already know:** *I want to … / I'd like to …*
And now: Future with *going to* – positive and negative statements

Lesson notes

Additional material
For optional and additional material for Unit 6, Step 1, see pages 94/95.
Refer to this section before your lesson as some of the materials require preparation.

Optional stages
Optional stages of the lesson are written in grey in these notes.

Photo page
5 mins

! Ask the class who the man is in the third photo. (James) If no-one remembers, ask them to look back at the photo on page 85.
- Students look at the photos on page 103 and answer the question. (Anna wants to give a presentation / say goodbye to her friends.)
- Refer students to *In dieser Unit lernen Sie u. a.:* … and give them time to read about what they're going to learn in Unit 6.

Starter: Speaking in public
5 mins

- Demonstrate the task by saying: *I spoke to a group of people last (Tuesday). There were about (12) people in the group and I talked about learning English.*
- ↓ Board:

  I spoke to a group of people about …
  I gave a presentation about …
  I made a speech about …

Anna's email
5+ mins

! This is the first time in Steps 1 and 2 that the main input is a text, rather than a dialogue. Give students time to read the email silently – it's better not to ask individuals to read it aloud as they are then faced with the added challenge of the pronunciation of new words.
- Remember to give students a small task before they read the text, e.g. *Which members of her family is Anna going to talk about in her presentation?*
- Students read the email and answer the question on the board. (grandparents, parents, brothers and sisters)
- Now read the mail to them so they become familiar with the new words.

Language and culture
The students can read the text *Emigration* (p. 119) and do the related task at home – or you can use this as a 'filler' if you have time at the end of the lesson. For more information on this, look at page 95 of this TRB.

1a Comprehension
5+ mins

- Alone (↓ or in pairs), students tick the correct information.

  ✓ 1, 4
- Volunteers correct the false information.
  2 … in the 1950s, 3 … about three generations, 5 … with Susan

1b Vocabulary: Putting information in order
5+ mins

- Students do the task alone (↓ or in pairs).

  First – First of all; Next – Then, After that, And then; And to finish – And finally

- To check the answers, have someone read out a sentence directly from the mail, e.g.
  First of all, *I'm going to start with some general information about my family.*
  Then ask a different student to repeat the sentence using the word / phrase from *Exercise 1b*:
  First, *I'm going to start with some general information about my family.*
  Do this for all the sentences:
  Then *I want to tell the class about Faversham in the 1940s. /*
  Next *I want to … .* ***After that,*** *I'm going to talk about my grandparents' live in Faversham. /*
  Next *I'm going to … .* ***And then*** *I want to say why my grandparents emigrated. /*
  Next *I want to … .* ***And finally,*** *I'd like to talk a bit about my parents. /*
  And to finish, *I'd like to …*

2a How to say it: Preparing a presentation

3/24
5+ mins

- Read out the phrases and have the class repeat them in chorus.
- In class, decide on where you'd use the phrases in a presentation.

1B, 2E, 3B, 4E, 5B, 6B

- Play ▶ 3/24 and students tick the phrases they hear.

✓ 2, 3, 4, 5

> (S = Susan, A = Anna)
> S: OK, Anna – now remember, nice and slowly …
> A: Good evening, everyone. My name's Anna Turner and this evening I'm going to tell you something about my family As you know, I'm from Canada but my family was from Faversham originally. So first of all, I'd like to show you my family tree and introduce you to my family. Then I'm going to tell you about Faversham in the 1940s – that's when my grandparents lived here. I'm going to show you some lovely old photos of the town and an old map. Then I'm going to tell you a bit about my grandparents' lives in Faversham – and we can look at some old letters that they wrote to friends here in England. Next, I'd like to talk about *why* they emigrated to Canada in the1950s. After that, I'd like to look at some statistics about British people emigrating to Canada. And finally, I'm going to tell you about my family today – my mother, who now lives in Quebec, and my brother and sister. So let's begin with this – my family tree …
> … as you can see in the photos. That's all for this evening. Thank you for listening. But, before we finish, do you have any questions?
> S: Well done, Anna! That was very good!

2b Anna's presentation

3/25
10– mins

- First ask an individual to read out the notes on the Post-its.
- Play ▶ 3/25. Students number the topics and check with a partner.

6, 2, 4; 3, 1, 5

- If necessary, play ▶ 3/25 again so they can confirm their answers.

3 Grammar
10 mins

NB: Up to now, students have been able to talk, in a limited way, about the future, using *I'd like to (do that tomorrow)* or *I want to (go there) after the lesson.* This is their first taste of a future tense. *Going to* was decided on because this is the tense used to talk about personal plans so it facilitates realistic communication.

You already know: *I want to … / I'd like to …*
! If some of your students are not very confident and want more revision practice, refer them to the *You already know* section of the *Language study* (p. 106). They can do the exercises in their book or online. Tell them to go to www.langenscheidt.de/networknow/selfstudy and type in the Language study code which is given at the top of page 106. Online they find – in addition to the exercises from their book – extra practice of the *You already know* grammar from *Network Now A1 Starter.*

And now: Future with *going to* – positive and negative statements

- Read out the sentences in the *And now* grammar box.

- Ask students to copy the information from the board but choose the correct last word(s) of the sentences.
  Board:
  These sentences with *going to* are about the present / past / future. (future)
  We can use *going to* to talk about every day / yesterday / next year. (next year)
- Show how to make *going to* sentences.
  Board:

I'm	going to	see him.
He's	going to	phone her.
They're	going to	mail me.

2a Say it like this
3/26
5 mins

- Explain and demonstrate that the *to* is not stressed in sentences with *going to* by reading out the sentences you wrote on the board.
- Refer students to the sentences in the *And now* grammar box. Play ▶ 3/26 and have the class repeat the sentences in chorus.

1 I'm going to talk about my grandparents.
2 Anna's going to show them some old photos.
3 She isn't going to talk about Canterbury.
4 They're going to look at an old map.

If short of time

If you notice you're getting short of time,
- do ***Exercise 3b*** orally, in class. Then students say what they can remember about other students.
- do just one of the ***Round up*** activities.

3b Now you: After your lesson
10 mins

- Demonstrate the activity by reading out three or four sentences about yourself – slightly stress the *not* in the negative sentences. Write a positive sentence and a negative sentence on the board.
  Board: I'm going to ... / I'm not going to ...
- Students complete the sentences about themselves and then tell a partner.

3c Now you: Your plans for next weekend
10 mins

- Point out the ***Info box*** and elicit sentences with *going to*. Ask: *Where's he going tomorrow?*
  He wants to watch a film tomorrow. (He's going to the cinema tomorrow.)
  He doesn't feel well. (He's going to the doctor's tomorrow.)
  He has to buy milk, apples and wine. (He's going to the supermarket tomorrow.)
  He's got a suitcase, a passport and a plane ticket. (He's going on holiday / to the airport tomorrow.)
- Follow coursebook instructions.

Round up
4a Next ...
5+ mins

- Demonstrate the activity by telling the class one of your plans for each of those times:
  I'm going to (visit my parents) next week.
  ! Encourage them to put the time on the end of the sentence by writing an example sentence on the board.

4b Your family
5+ mins

- Follow coursebook instructions.

And finally ...
5+ mins

Remind students of the following:
- **Language study** (p. 106): Students can do this in the book or online. Tell them to go to www.langenscheidt.de/networknow/selfstudy and type in the Language study code which is given at the top of page 106. Online they find – in addition to the exercises from their book – extra practice of the *You already know* grammar from *Network Now A1 Starter*.
- **Selfstudy** (p. 107): Students can do this in the book or online.
- **Keys** (p. 131) to the Language study and Selfstudy exercises.
- **Language and culture**, Step 1: *Emigration* and the corresponding task (p. 119).

And point out ...
- the **Lerntipp** on how to practise their English during the break before the next course will start.

Unit 6 Step 2 The last evening

Contents

Storyline It's the last evening of the family history course and the students go to a restaurant with Dave.
Functions Asking about future plans; Saying goodbye
Vocabulary Verbs with prepositions *(look at, talk about, listen to, ...); later, next weekend*
Grammar **You already know:** Future with *going to* – positive and negative statements (see Unit 6 Step 1)
And now: Future with *going to* – questions and short answers

Lesson notes

Additional material
For optional and additional material for Unit 6, Step 2, see page 95.
Refer to this section before your lesson as some of the materials require preparation.

Optional stages
Optional stages of the lesson are written in grey in these notes.

Starter: Your plans
5 mins
- Demonstrate the activity by giving the class a false piece of information about what you're going to do at the weekend. Invite individual students to say if it's true or false. Then students make their own sentences.

What are you going to do?
3/31
10 mins
- Ask students to cover the dialogue. Read out the introduction to the dialogue and then ask: *What do you think they're going to talk about?* Write the suggestions on the board.
- Play ▶ 3/31 and tick off any topics that they talk about.
- Play ▶ 3/31 again so that students can check the answers. (Anna's presentation, Mrs Benton, Anna's mother, the course, the next course, Anna's return to Faversham)

Tip: Personalisation (2) Students will find it easier to remember structures and vocabulary if they make sentences relevant to themselves. For example, in the dialogue, Anna says *Faversham is my second home*. Invite students to make a sentence, replacing the place name. Give an example: *I live in Munich but Berlin is my second home.*

Language and culture
The students can read the text *Immigration* (p. 119) and do the related tasks at home – or you can use this as a 'filler' if you have time at the end of the lesson. For more information on this, look at page 95 of this TRB.

1a Comprehension
5 mins
- Students answer the questions in class.

1 She's going to copy them and make a book for her mother. 2 They learned a lot about their families. / They enjoyed it. 3 They're going to do a project on families who emigrated to Australia in the 1950s. 4 Anna has to go back to Canada next week. 5 Yes, she is. / Of course she is.

1b Vocabulary: Verbs with prepositions
10+ mins
- **!** We can't expect all students to know what a verb + preposition means, so write two examples from the text.
Board:
Anna's happy Mrs Benton didn't throw the letters __________. (away)
Anna isn't going to give them __________. (back)
- Alone (↓ or in pairs), students write in the missing prepositions.
1 for, 2 to, 3 for, 4 to, 5 at, 6 to, 7 about
- Check the answers by having volunteers read out the correct answers.

- Do the second part of the exercise as a class activity, asking volunteers to make alternative endings to the sentences.
  Example sentences:
  Before she leaves, Anna's going to look for her tickets / Canadian money / keys. She's going to say goodbye to James / Mrs Benton. She's going to buy a present for Dave / Susan and Tom. On the plane Anna's going to listen to her iPlayer / guitar music. She's going to look at photos of her class / Canterbury. She's going to talk to the flight attendant / other people. She's going to talk about Canada / her family.

2 Grammar
5– mins

You already know: Future with *going to* – positive and negative sentences
! If some of your students are not very confident and want more revision practice, refer them to the *You already know* section of the *Language study* (p. 110). They can do the exercises in their book or online. Tell them to go to www.langenscheidt.de/networknow/selfstudy and type in the Language study code which is given at the top of page 110. Online they find – in addition to the exercises from their book – extra practice of the *You already know* grammar from *Network Now A1 Starter.*

And now: Future with *going to* (questions and short answers)
- Read out the questions and short answers from the *And now* grammar box and have the class repeat them in chorus.
- Ask questions to different students. They should reply using *Yes, I am* or *No, I'm not.*
  Are you going to … after the lesson?
  do your homework, drive home, go home by taxi, go to a restaurant, meet friends, have a cigarette, watch TV, drink a beer, phone a friend, check your emails

2a Now you: What are you going to do?
10– mins

- Practise the phrases by asking individuals to ask the questions and choose one of the times to put on the end of the question.
- ↓ Students can write down three questions, each with a different time on the end.
- Point out the ***Info box*** – this gives a repeated reminder about *going to + go* (see the *Info box* in Step 1) – this is relevant for the last two questions in the list.
- Demonstrate the activity with an able student.

! Remind students to give the short answer *Yes, I am* or *No I'm not* – not just *Yes* or *No*, as a one word answer sounds very abrupt in English.

2b Tell the class
5 mins

- Follow coursebook instructions.

3a How to say it: Talking about the future
5 mins

- **!** Here there are four possible ways of talking about the future. Only one, the *going to* form, expresses a definite plan.

4

If short of time

If you notice you're getting short of time,
- do ***Exercise 3b*** as a class activity with each student contributing just one sentence.
- do just one of the ***Round up*** activities.

3b Now you: Your future
10– mins

- Follow coursebook instructions.

4a How to say it: Saying goodbye
5+ mins

- Students write in the missing words.

1 see, 2 Have, 3 holiday, 4 forget, 5 soon
- Read out the completed sentences and have the class repeat them in chorus.

4b Anna says goodbye
3/32
5+ mins

- Ask students to speculate about who Anna says gooodbye to: *She might say goodbye to …*
- Play ▶ 3/32.

1 Dave, 2 Susan, 3 Mrs Benton, 4 James

1 ... and thanks for everything. Your course was really interesting. I learned a lot. You have my email address so we can stay in contact. Well, goodbye – and have a nice holiday and good luck with the next course.
2 ... and I had lots of fun with you – shopping together, doing the course – and the lovely dinners at your place. Well, this is goodbye. I hope you and Tom are going to visit me in Canada next year. I'd love to see you.
3 Thanks again for those lovely photos and letters. I'm going to show them to my mother when I'm home. And don't forget to write to me when I'm back in Ottawa.
4 It was good of you to drive me to the airport. You know, I had a great time here in England. And the last weeks were the best, thanks to you. It was so lucky that I asked *you* the way in Kew! So – maybe see you in the summer ...

Round up
5a Goodbye, Anna
5+ mins

! In this activity, students practise talking about the past, the present and the future. They say what Anna did in Faversham; what she wants to do before leaving Faversham; and speculate about what she's going to do in the future.

5b Say goodbye
5– mins

- Follow coursebook instructions.

And finally ...
5+ mins

Remind students of the following:
- **Language study** (p. 110): Students can do this in the book or online. Tell them to go to www.langenscheidt.de/networknow/selfstudy and type in the Language study code which is given at the top of page 110. Online they find – in addition to the exercises from their book – extra practice of the *You already know* grammar from *Network Now A1 Starter.*
- **Selfstudy** (p. 111): Students can do this in the book or online.
- **Keys** (p. 131) to the Language study and Selfstudy exercises.
- **Language and culture,** Step 2: *Immigration* and the corresponding tasks (p. 119). Encourage students to do the Internet task at home.

Unit 6 Step 3 The end of term

Contents

Realia	An appointment card
Functions	Making an appointment
Vocabulary	Homophones
Reading	False teeth
Grammar	Review of tenses – present, past, future

Lesson notes

Additional material

For optional and additional material for Unit 6, Step 3, see page 96.
Refer to this section before your lesson as some of the materials require preparation.

Optional stages

Optional stages of the lesson are written in grey in these notes.

Starter: During the break
5– mins

- Demonstrate the activity by telling the class some of your plans for the end of term break. Use *going to* to talk about your plans.
- Individual students tell the class about their plans. Encourage the class to ask questions to elicit more details.

An appointment
1a Dave's appointment
5+ mins

- Give students time to read the appointment card and remind them that it isn't necessary to understand every word in order to get the information they need. Then, in class, they ask and answer the questions.
  1 He's going to (go to) the dentist's during the summer break. 2 His dentist is AJ Turnbull. 3 His dentist's is in Canterbury. 4 His appointment is on Thursday, August 11th, at 2pm.
- Point out the ***Info box*** about *dentist* = *the person; dentist's* = *the place.*

Language and culture

The students can read the text *Dates* (p. 119) and do the related task at home – or you can use this as a 'filler' if you have time at the end of the lesson. For more information on this, look at page 96 of this TRB.

1b How to make an appointment
3/37
10– mins

- Give students time to read through the dialogue before they listen to it and tick the phrases they hear. Play ▶ 3/37.

✓ Good morning, I'd like, Tuesday, I don't have time, What about, fine, afternoon at 3, earlier, earlier, OK, Right, Thanks a lot, Goodbye

(R = Receptionist, D = Dave)
R: Ashby Dental Surgery. Good morning. Can I help you?
D: Hello. This is Dave Evans. I'd like to make an appointment, please – just for a check-up.
R: Right. Would Tuesday be OK?
D: I'm sorry, I don't have time then.
R: What about Thursday?
D: Yes, Thursday's fine.
R: Thursday afternoon at 3?
D: Oh, do you have anything earlier?
R: Yes, one hour earlier?
D: Yes, that's OK for me.
R: Right. I have your email address so I can send you your appointment card.
D: Thanks a lot. See you then. Bye.
R: You're welcome. Goodbye.

1c Act it out
10– mins

- In pairs, students act out the two dialogues.
- Volunteers can perform a dialogue for the class.

1d Now you: Your appointments
10 mins

- First demonstrate the activity by telling the class about one of your appointments.
- **!** Point out the ***Info box*** about *appointment* being used for official, not social, meetings.
  NB: A boyfriend / girlfriend meeting is a *date*. At work, you have a *meeting*. And a social meeting with a friend? *I'm going to meet (Anna).*

2 Grammar: Review of tenses
5+ mins

NB: In this, the last Step 3 of *Network Now A1*, there is no new grammatical structure. Instead, there's an overview of the three main tenses that students have practised in this book (present simple, past simple, future with *going to*) – this makes it clear to the students that they are now able to talk about their past, present and future.

- Have the students read the sentences in the grammar box in preparation for *Exercise 2a*.

2a Dental check-ups
3/38
5 mins

- ↓ Board:
  He has a check-up once a year.
  He had his last check-up twelve months ago.
  He's going to have his next check-up next August.
- Play ▶ 3/38 and students correct the sentences in the grammar box.
  ! Warn students that the information they hear is in a different order from the sentences in the grammar box.
- Play ▶ 3/38 again so that students can check their answers.
  He has a check-up ~~once a year~~ **every six months.** He had his last check-up ~~twelve months ago~~ **six months ago.** He's going to have his next check-up next ~~August~~ **February.**

> (T = Mr Turnbull, dentist, D = Dave)
> T: Well, Mr Evans – no problems there. Excellent teeth! Er – when was your last check-up?
> D: Oh, when was that? I think I had a check-up last February. It was about six months ago. I usually have a check-up every six months.
> T: Excellent! So – see you again in six months?
> D: That's right, see you next February. Thanks very much Mr Turnbull. Bye.

2b Now you: Your dental appointments
5 mins

- Follow coursebook instructions.

Reading: False teeth
5+ mins

FYI: The 1966 World Cup is still a hotly discussed topic among football fans! England beat Germany 4 – 2 in the World Cup final at Wembley Stadium in London. After 90 minutes, the score was 2 – 2 and the teams had to play extra time. Geoff Hurst scored England's third goal – but it's debateable whether the ball crossed the goal line or not. Then, in the final seconds of the game, Geoff Hurst scored England's fourth goal, making it the first time England had won the Jules Rimet Trophy.

If short of time

If you notice you're getting short of time,

- choose just two or three of the people in ***Exercise 3a*** and ask students to give details about them.

3a Remember the text
5 mins

Tip: Correction (3) Of course, when practising structures, the focus is on accuracy and students need correction. But in some cases, as in *Exercise 3a*, the focus is on conveying information and it's more important for the student to 'get the message across' than to be 100% accurate in doing so. In these cases, only correct the student when the mistake gets in the way of communication, otherwise the student could become too inhibited to venture to speak.

- Let your students decide for themselves how challenging they want this activity to be.
  Board:
  * Leave the text uncovered.
  ** As in the coursebook. Say one thing you can remember about each person.
  *** Make two sentences about each person.
- Follow coursebook instructions.

3b Find words that sound the same
10+ mins

NB: This exercise relies on standard British pronunciation. But it doesn't harm students to be made aware that teachers may have regional accents and pronounce words differently from 'standard' English. And this is beneficial for the students because when they use their English outside the classroom, it's unlikely that they will speak only to native English speakers using standard pronunciation.

- Alone (↓ or in pairs), students look through the text to find the homophones.
  to, too; for; no; won; their
- Check the answers by having individual students read out the sentence containing the word. Example sentences:
  1789 – 1797 George Washington: And he was famous for his false teeth, too;
  1966 World Cup: All the players remembered to put in their false teeth before they met the Queen ...;
  2008: Eight British students created the first set of false teeth for cats;
  Today: There is still an old law in America that says that no married woman in Vermont can wear false teeth ...;
  1966: England won the World Cup;
  1966 World Cup: All the players remembered to put in their false teeth ...
- Then students make their own sentences with the homophones.

Time for a game
4 Present, past and future
10+ mins

! This game gives students the opportunity to make sentences about anything they choose, but directs them to use structures to practise the past, present and future.

- Ideally, this game should be played in pairs, but it can be played in groups of three if you have an odd number of students in the class.
- Each student needs a marker – a small coin, for example. The rules are simple. Give students time to read through them before they place their markers – one in an orange circle and one in a green circle.

And finally ...
5– mins

Remind students of the following:

- **Language study** (p. 114): Students can do this in the book or online.
- **Selfstudy** (p. 114): Students can do this in the book or online.
- **Keys** (p. 131) to the Language study and Selfstudy exercises.
- **Language and culture,** Step 3: *Dates* and the corresponding task (p. 119).

And point out ...

3/40

- **Reading: What am I going to do?** (p. 115): A song to be sung 'just for fun'. There's a glossary of unknown words and the song is also recorded so it's easy to sing along. For more information on this, look at pages 96 and 121 of this TRB.

Unit 6 Now I can

Contents — **Review of vocabulary, functions and structures in Unit 6**

Storyline	The people in Alun's German course meet for an end-of-term drink and they talk about plans for the summer.
Starter	Talking about future plans
Part 1	Talking about future plans; Structuring ideas; Preparing a short presentation
Part 2	Talking about future plans; Making an appointment
Part 3	Talking about future plans; Asking about other people's plans; Saying goodbye

Lesson notes

Additional material

For optional and additional material for Unit 6, *Now I can*, see pages 96/97.
Refer to this section before your lesson as some of the materials require preparation.

Optional stages

Optional stages of the lesson are written in grey in these notes.

Jetzt kann ich u. a.: ...
5– mins

- Ask students to look at *Jetzt kann ich u. a.: ...* Remind them that the symbols refer to different skills or vocabulary items which they learnt in Unit 6 and were listed in the aims on the photo page (p. 103). Most of the tasks in *Now I can* focus on more than one skill or vocabulary item.

Starter: The future ... after Unit 6
10– mins

- First elicit the names of the people in the photos. (Anna, Dave, Susan and Tom, Mrs Benton, James)
- ↓ Give prompts if students don't have enough ideas.
  Anna: Canada – mother – James
  Dave: dentist's – Canada – course
  Susan and Tom: holiday – next course – Anna
  Mrs Benton: Canada – letters – photos
  James: fly – job – emails
  Example answers: **Anna's going to return to Canada. She isn't going to attend the next course. She might come back to England. Dave's going to the dentist's in August. He's going organise a project about Australia. Susan and Tom might visit Anna in Canada. They're going to Dave's next course. Mrs Benton isn't going to visit Anna in Canada. She's going to write to her. James might have a holiday in Canada. He's going to stay in contact with Anna.**

Part 1:
1a What are you going to present?
10 mins

- If you can't make groups of four, have one or two groups of three and ask the most able person in each group to take the role of two people.
- The group chooses a town they all know. Monitor this part of the activity to help with ideas if necessary.
- ↑ If you have a very able group, encourage them to think of more unusual places, e.g. Disneyland, a ghost town, Dodge City – and, if it happens to be Christmas, Santa's town in the North Pole.

1b A presentation about Zurich
3/41
15+ mins

- First have the class speculate about what the students might talk about (lakes, tourism, banks, languages, etc.). Write the list on the board.
- Play ▶ 3/41 and tick off any of the topics which are talked about.
- Read the instruction for 1b and ask students to fill in the information. Play ▶ 3/41 again.
- After the task, pool the information by asking individuals to read out the notes they made.
  1 The city – a map, 2 The lake and mountains – photo of a boat, 3 The art museum – postcards, 4 Carnival – photos of costumes

(A–D = students in the German class)
1
A: We're going to tell you about our city – the city where we all live, Zurich. First I'm going to tell you about the city, the number of people who live here and where they live. I'm going to show you a map of Zurich.
2
B: Then I'm going to tell you about the lake and the mountains. You can see both of these – from the city, from the middle of the city. I'm going to show you a picture of a big boat on the lake. You can go on trips on this boat.
3
C: After that I'm going to talk a little bit about the art museum in Zurich. It's a big museum and has a very good collection. I'm going to show you some postcards from the special exhibitions of the last few years, for example ... Picasso and Cezanne.
4
D: And finally, I'm going to talk about something very important in Zurich – no ... not the banks ... I'm going to talk about carnival time. We have a very special kind of music at this time, it's called 'Guggemusik'. I'm going to play you some Guggemusik ... and show you some photos of carnival costumes.
And this is going to be the end of our presentation.

1c Plan your presentation
10 mins

- Encourage the groups to make notes on paper, in a similar way to the way they did it in *Exercise 1b*: Topic: ... Show: ... .
- Monitor the activity, prompting with ideas if necessary.

1d Introduce your presentation
10 mins

- Point out the phrases that the four students use in the speech bubbles. Suggest that they each write down on their paper the phrase they need to use.
- Invite a group to come to the front of the class – with their papers – and present their ideas to the class.

Tip: Encouragement We must remember that a lot of students are unused to speaking in public and may have to overcome shyness and inhibitions. When students are giving their presentations in *Exercise 1d*, only interrupt if absolutely necessary, e.g. if they get really stuck for words – but don't correct them. Promote an encouraging atmosphere and give a round of applause after each group has finished.

Part 2:
2a More information
5+ mins

- Students need to decide on a topic for their presentation that they need more information about. If some groups need more help with ideas, suggest:
  airport – you want an appointment with someone on the information desk to ask about lost property statistics
  music festival – you want an appointment with the organiser to ask about the schedules and artists.
  museum – you want an appointment with the director to ask about their new exhibition
  sports centre – you want an appointment with the receptionist to ask about the sports + facilities they offer
  farmer's market / flea market – you want an appointment with the local organiser to ask about how sellers can get a stall.

2b Make the appointment
10+ mins

- Ask half the class to take their books and stand together on one side of the room – they are the A students and should look at page 123. The other half, the B students, should stand together on the other side of the room and look at page 124. Give students a few minutes to read what they have to do and, if necessary, ask each other questions to clarify the instructions.
- Students choose a partner from their group and then team up with a pair from the other group.

NB: Organising an A/B activity in this way has several advantages: students easily find the right page; they can ask each other questions if the instructions aren't clear to them; and they will work with a different partner, not simply the person next to them.

- In pairs, students perform the task. Then they perform it to the other pair in their group of four.

Part 3:
3a The future

3/42
5+ mins

! Tell students that when they take notes, they shouldn't try to write down whole sentences, only reminders. Point out the two examples in the book.

- Students listen and take notes on the things the students asked about. Play ▶ 3/42 – twice, if necessary.
  1 holiday next summer, 2 German-speaking country, 3 next course, 4 here at Christmas, 5 concert – weekend / music festival – summer

> (Al = Alun, A–D = students in the German class)
> Al: What are you going to do in the summer? Are you going to have a holiday?
> A: Erm, I'm going to have a holiday from work, but I'm going to stay at home ... in my garden.
>
> Al: Are you gong to visit a German-speaking country in the future ... to practise your German?
> B: Hmmm – yes, that's a good idea. Are you going to do that?
>
> Al: Are you going to come to the next course?
> C: Yes, I am.
> D: I'm not going to come ... I can't. I'm going to learn Spanish ... it's for my job.
>
> A: Alun, are you going to be here at Christmas?
> Al: Yes, I am ... why do you ask?
> A: Well, I thought we could ...
>
> D: Are you going to the concert this weekend?
> C: No, I'm not – I don't have a ticket. But I'm going to the music festival in the summer. Are you?
> D: Oh yes, of course I'm going ... I always go ... every year.

If short of time

The **final activity** of the *Now I can* pages allows for time flexibility as it's often an open-ended activity. You can limit the amount of time spent on the walk around phase of ***Exercise 3b***.

3b The end of the course
5+ mins

- ↓ Before students walk around and ask questions, have volunteers make questions with the notes they made in *Exercise 3a*.
- Join in this final walk and talk activity in which students ask each other questions about the forthcoming break and say goodbye to people in their course.

And finally ...
5 mins

Remind students of the following:

- **Test yourself** (p. 118): Students can assess their progress by doing this test and checking their answers (p. 131).
- **Language and culture** (p. 119): Refer your students to any *L&C* texts and tasks that weren't read or done in class.
- **Now me** (p. 120): Students can personalise their learning by writing short texts and noting down vocabulary which is particularly useful to them. Advise them to keep a record of their progress by assembling a dossier. Refer them to www.langenscheidt.de/networknow/portfolio.
- At the end of the lesson, say goodbye to each student individually – and say that you hope to see them in the next course, *Network Now A2.1*.

Does your course have more than the standard 24 lessons?

- After Unit 6, there is the optional section **Globetrotter:**
  Globetrotter C Work – one page (45 minutes) of classroom material with the focus on English for work.
  Globetrotter C Travel – one page (45 minutes) of classroom material with the focus on English for travel.
  A further 45 minutes of classroom material is provided on the Internet for this lesson.
  Teaching notes on **Globetrotter C** can also be found on pages 125/126.

Your notes

Note: Getting ready for ... is divided into two sections, **FYI** and **Preparing ...**, for most of the steps in Units 1–6.

FYI: When you prepare your lessons, you might want to have some background knowledge of an aspect of the lesson – just for your own personal interest. Where it seems useful, the FYI provides links to relevant sites via the *Network Now* homepage.

Preparing ...: If your lesson is longer than 90 minutes, or if you have a particularly quick class, this section offers some additional activities which you can use. Some of the activities and materials require some preparation before the lesson.

Getting ready for Unit 1

FYI Unit 1 Step 1

You can find out more about **Faversham**, where the story takes place, by going to www.langenscheidt.de/networknow/fyi.

Preparing Unit 1 Step 1

Likes and dislikes chain
10 mins

- To be used any time after *Exercise 2b*, coursebook p. 11.
- Students write six sentences, using each of the positive and negative phrases in *Exercise 2b*. The sentences can be completed with hobbies, food, cities, etc.
- Start the activity by saying: *I love (Indian food). What about you?* Students can respond by saying: *I love (Indian food), too* or *I don't like (Indian food).*
- The student who has answered then addresses another student and reads out one of his / her sentences and asks: *What about you?* Continue the chain until everyone in the class has said at least one sentence.

In my bag ...
15– mins

- To be used any time after *Exercise 3a* or in place of *Exercise 3b*, coursebook p. 11.
  NB: This activity takes about 10 minutes longer than *Exercise 3b*.
- **Photocopy** ***1 In my bag ...*** (p. 98) – one for each student.
- Students work in pairs and label the photos.
  NB: New words – *coins, letter, sweets*
- Then they try to make a row of four (horizontal, vertical or diagonal) by saying what they have in their bags.

Language and culture Step 1: Ottawa
(coursebook p. 25)
10– mins

- To be used after the *Round up*, coursebook p. 11.
- Allow time for students to read the text silently.
- Ask if any student has any more information about Canada – maybe someone has been there or has family or friends there.
- **!** When doing the task, invite contributions from students who are not from the local area.

Downloads

- There's an activity for Unit 1 Step 1 which you can download from the Internet: www.langenscheidt.de/networknow/activities

And finally ...

If you haven't used the *Zero lesson*, photocopy the *Learner profile* (p. 7) – one for each student and ask them to fill it in as part of their homework.

FYI Unit 1 Step 2

If you'd like to go on a virtual tour of **Canterbury Cathedral**, go to www.langenscheidt.de/networknow/fyi.

Preparing Unit 1 Step 2

Running dictation
10 mins

- To be used any time after the dialogue, coursebook p. 14.
- **Photocopy** ***2 Running dictation*** (p. 99) and cut it into three sections.
- Say to the students: *Let's write a dictation. You need paper and a pen.*
- Put the class into three groups, A, B and C and get them to sit together in their groups.
- Choose the most able and confident student in each group as the 'runner'.
- Stand the texts in three different places in the room and tell each group which text is theirs.
- The 'runner' has to leave the group, read a sentence (or two) of the group's text, remember it and 'run' back to the group and dictate the sentence(s).
- When all the groups have finished, one member from each group reads out the text and a member from another group checks it with the original.

NB: It's more fun if you can place the texts in different places outside the classroom and the groups have a competition to see which group finishes first!

What do you think of it?
15 mins

- An alternative to *Exercise 4b*, coursebook p. 15.
- Cut pieces of DIN A4 paper into small rectangles (4 x 6) – one sheet of paper makes 24 rectangles.

You need enough for 6 rectangles for each student in your class.

- Hand out 6 rectangles to each student.
- Ask students to write the following things on the six pieces of paper.

Board: 1 the name of a TV personality, 2 the name of a city, 3 something to eat, 4 a sort of music, 5 a hobby, 6 something to drink

- Students get into pairs and put their rectangles together in a pile.
- Each pair of students swaps their pile with another pair.
- Students do the activity set out in *Exercise 4b*, but instead of choosing items from the list, they turn over a rectangle.

Language and culture Step 2: Canterbury
(coursebook p. 25)
10– mins

- To be used after the *Round up*, coursebook p. 15.
- Allow time for students to read the text silently.
- **!** When doing the task, invite contributions from students who are not from this country.
- Encourage the students to do the Internet activity at home.

Downloads

- There's an activity for Unit 1 Step 2 which you can download from the Internet: www.langenscheidt.de/networknow/activities

FYI Unit 1 Step 3

To read more about strange **lost property** go to www.langenscheidt.de/networknow/fyi.

Preparing Unit 1 Step 3

Famous people
15– mins

- To be used any time after *Exercise 1c*, coursebook p. 18.
- **Photocopy** ***3 Famous people*** (p. 100) – one for each pair of students and cut it in half, A and B.
- Students work in pairs, A and B, and follow the instructions on the paper.

Lost property chain game
10 mins

- To be used any time after *Exercise 4b*, coursebook p. 19.
- Begin the chain by saying: *I lost my mobile phone.* A student continues: *I lost my mobile phone and my (keys).* The third student repeats what was said and adds one more item, etc.

Language and culture Step 3: Titles
(coursebook p. 25)
10– mins

- To be used at the end of the lesson.
- Allow time for students to read the text silently.
- Ask each student to say his / her title in English.
- After doing the task, ask if the students know any other famous people with the titles: *Mr, Dr, Mrs* or *Miss.*

Reading: At the Lost Property Office
(coursebook p. 21)

- The Reading page can be done as selfstudy or read in class. You'll find ideas on how to exploit this in class on page 119.

Downloads

- There's an activity for Unit 1 Step 3 which you can download from the Internet: www.langenscheidt.de/networknow/activities

FYI Unit 1 Now I can

Alun's name is Welsh. Did you know, there is a colony of Welsh speakers in Argentina? Find out more about the **Welsh language** and listen to a Welsh speaker by going to www.langenscheidt.de/networknow/fyi.

Preparing Unit 1 Now I can

Note: As the *Now I can* pages are revision and consolidation, you can use any of the optional and additional materials suggested for Steps 1–3.

Repeat and complete
5+ mins

- To be used with *Exercise 3*, coursebook p. 23.
- When the students have read the text about Alun silently, ask them to cover the text and repeat and complete the following sentences.
- *Alan Burton works in a* (hotel). *He's the assistant* (manager). *He interviews people for* (jobs). *He works from 8.30 to* (5 o'clock). *Twice a month he works at the* (weekend). *A lot of tourists come from different* (countries). *So Alun's job is really* (interesting).

Template 1: A form
10+ mins

- To be used after *Exercise 3*, coursebook p. 23.
- **Photocopy Template 1:** ***A form*** (p. 113) – so that, when you've cut the page in two, you have one form for each student.
- In class, students interview the teacher (or each other). In turns, they ask questions to elicit information which can be written on the forms. (Remember – the information need not be true!)

Downloads

- There's an activity for Unit 1 *Now I can* which you can download from the Internet: www.langenscheidt.de/networknow/activities

Getting ready for Unit 2

Preparing Unit 2 Step 1

Times
5 mins

- To be used any time after *Exercise 2a*, coursebook p. 28.
- For extra practice, say: *In Britain, they are one hour behind Germany. Look at clock number 1 in Exercise 2a. What time is it here? What's the time in England?*

Writing competition
10 mins

- To be used any time after *Exercise 3*, coursebook p. 29.
- Remind students that the 'how often' words go before the verb: *I often get up early* and 'how often' phrases go at the end of the sentence: *I get up early once a month*. Write the two sentences on the board: I often get up early.
  I get up early once a month.

- Tell students they have five minutes to write as many sentences as they can, adding 'how often' words and phrases to the sentence on the board: Tony eats pizza.
- After five minutes, have a student read out his / her sentences – the other students cross out the sentences they hear read out. The next student reads out his / her remaining sentences, and so on.

How often do they do that?
10 mins

- To be used any time after *Exercise 3b*, coursebook p. 29.
- Look at the activity *How often do they do that?* on page 101. In the three empty squares (*), fill in three names of living people who are in the news at the moment – a sportsperson, a politician, an entertainer etc.
- **Photocopy *4 How often do they do that?*** (p. 101) – one for each pair of students.
- Cut out the squares and make 2 separate sets for each pair of students – *Who?* and *How often?*
- In pairs, students put the piles, face down, on their desk. In turn, they turn over a *Who?* card and a *How often?* card and make a sentence with the words, beginning with: *I think that ...*
- Demonstrate the activity a couple of times so that students get the idea.

Language and culture Step 1: Time
(coursebook p. 43)
10– mins

- To be used after the *Round up*, coursebook p. 29.
- Ask around the class: *What time do you get up / go to bed / start work?*
- Allow time for students to read the text silently.
- Invite students to speculate on the meanings of the 'time' phrases.
- When doing the task, invite contributions from students who are not from this country – accept answers in German if the English is too complex.

Downloads

- There's an activity for Unit 2 Step 1 which you can download from the Internet: www.langenscheidt.de/networknow/activities

Preparing Unit 2 Step 2

About the text
5+ mins

- To be used any time after *Exercise 1a*, coursebook p. 32.
- Students cover the text.
- Write the following prompt words on the board and ask individual students to make a sentence using information from the dialogue: Tom – Saturday – London – Mrs Benton – grandmother

NB: You can do this as a writing exercise but it will take about three times as long.

Complete the sentences
5 mins

- To be used any time after *Exercise 2*, coursebook p. 32.
- Board: go out, going out, to go out
- Ask individual students to repeat what you say and complete the sentences with a phrase from the board: *Shall we* (go out)? *Would you like* (to go out)? *How about* (going out)? *I'd like* (to go out). *Let's* (go out). *I'd love* (to go out). *Why don't we* (go out)? *I can't* (go out).

Questions
15– mins

- To be used any time after *Exercise 3b*, coursebook p. 33.
- **Photocopy *5 Questions*** (p. 102) – one for each pair of students.
- In pairs, students read the instructions and play the game.

Language and culture Step 2: Free time
(coursebook p. 43)
10– mins

- To be used after the *Round up*, coursebook p. 33.
- Ask around the class: *What's your main free time activity? Do you often cook for friends? Where do you meet your friends? Do you do other courses or just English? Which sports do you do? Are you in a club? What's your main hobby? Do you spend a lot of time reading? How often do you watch television?*
- Ask: *How much of his / her free time does a typical English person spend watching TV? More than 10%? More than 30%? More than 40%?*
- Repeat the numbers and ask for a show of hands. Then say: *Let's find out the answer. Look at page 43, Step 2 – Free time.*
- Allow time for students to read the text silently.
- Ask students to think about their country and to write down what they think the percentages are. These can be checked on the Internet at home if they follow the *Network Now* link on page 43.

Downloads

- There's an activity for Unit 2 Step 2 which you can download from the Internet: www.langenscheidt.de/networknow/activities

FYI Unit 2 Step 3

If you'd like to know more about **English pub names**, go to www.langenscheidt.de/networknow/fyi.

Preparing Unit 2 Step 3

Comprehension
5 mins

- To be used any time after *Exercise 2a*, coursebook p. 36.
- Read the Reading text, *Molly Malone*, aloud to the class.
- In pairs, students write four sentences about the text on a piece of paper – they can be true or false – give them an example.
  Board: Molly Malone was American. T / F (False)
- Students swap papers with another pair of students and say if the sentences are true or false.

Crossword
15– mins

- To be used any time after *Exercise 3b*, coursebook p. 37.
- **Photocopy *6 Crossword*** (p. 103) – one for each pair of students. Cut off the lower half of the paper and give each partner his / her half of the crossword with the corresponding instructions.
- In pairs, students read the instructions on their paper and complete their half of the crossword by asking their partner for clues.

1 V	I	2 P						3 M		4 I
		U		5 D		6 G	H	O	S	T
7 D	U	B	L	I	N			L		A
I				A		8 T		L		L
N		9 K	E	N	N	E	D	Y		Y
N				A		A			10 B	
E						11 M	U	S	I	C
12 R	O	M	E						K	
					13 W	I	N	N	E	R

Language and culture Step 3: Pubs
(coursebook p. 43)
10– mins

- To be used at the end of the lesson.
- Allow time for students to read the text silently.
- Ask students what the differences are between English pubs and German *Gasthäuser*.
  (pub signs, different types of food, order at the bar – pay immediately, pints not litres, buying rounds, say *Cheers*)

Reading: Quiz time – riddles
(coursebook p. 39)

- The Reading page can be done as selfstudy or read in class. You'll find ideas on how to exploit this in class on pages 119/120.

Downloads

- There's an activity for Unit 2 Step 3 which you can download from the Internet:
  www.langenscheidt.de/networknow/activities

Preparing Unit 2 Now I can

Note: As the *Now I can* pages are revision and consolidation, you can use any of the optional and additional materials suggested for Steps 1–3.

Template 2: Clocks
10+ mins

- To be used any time after the *Starter* exercise, coursebook p. 40.
- **Photocopy Template 2: *Clocks*** (p. 114) – so that you have one sheet of paper for each student.

- There is a variety of activities that you can use these clocks for:

  Clocks A – H
  1. Get students to ask each other the time, e.g. *Clock A. What's the time (Sarah)?*
  2. Tell students that the time in London is one hour earlier and the time in Bucharest is one hour later. Get students to ask each other: *It's (2 o'clock) in Berlin. What's the time in London / Bucharest?*
  3. Say: *My watch is ten minutes fast / slow. Look at clock A. What's the time on my watch?*
  4. Indicate a clock and read out the time in numbers, and add *am* or *pm*, e.g. *It's (eight twenty) am / pm* and students respond: *It's (twenty past eight) in the morning / afternoon / evening.*
  5. Students say what they often do at these times.

  Clocks I – P
  Dictate times for students to draw in the clocks.

Five guesses
10+ mins

- To be used after *Exercise 3b*, coursebook p. 41.
- Individual students tell the class the answer to one of the questions in *Exercise 3a* – but leave out the key phrase.
- Demonstrate the activity by answering the first sentence: *I eat one ... a day.*
- Invite the class to ask you questions beginning with *Do you ...?* to find out the missing phrase: *Do you eat one orange a day? / Do you eat one piece of toast a day?* etc.
- After five guesses, tell them the answer.

Downloads

- There's an activity for Unit 2 *Now I can* which you can download from the Internet: www.langenscheidt.de/networknow/activities

Getting ready for Unit 3

FYI Unit 3 Step 1

If you'd like to find out more about **Charles and Diana's wedding day**, go to www.langenscheidt.de/networknow/fyi.

Preparing Unit 3 Step 1

Word search
10 mins

- To be used any time after *Exercise 2b*, coursebook p. 49.
- **Photocopy *7 Wordsearch*** (p. 104) – one for each student.
- In pairs, students find the past tenses of the remaining twelve verbs and write the infinitive and the past form on the paper.
  horizontal →: **write – wrote**
  vertical ↓: **wear – wore, buy – bought, make – made, see – saw, go – went, come – came**
  diagonal ↘: **send – sent, take – took, know – knew, give – gave**
  diagonal ↗: **meet – met, get – got**
- If you have more time, ask them to make sentences with the past forms.

Clothes chain game
5+ mins

- To be used any time after *Exercise 3b*, coursebook p. 49.
- Start off the chain by saying: *I went on holiday and I packed a red jacket.*
- Nominate a student to repeat your sentence and add another item of clothing: *I went on holiday and I packed a red jacket and ...* . Continue round the class.

Tip: Playing cards There are lots of simple strategies to add variety to your lessons. Take a pack of 52 playing cards into your classroom.

Use the cards for group + pairwork
You can use the cards to make sure your students work with different partners / groups.

- If you want your class to do an A / B activity, you need an equal number of red cards and black cards, and the same number of cards as you have students in the class. Deal out the cards and students who get a red card form one group, the holders of black cards make the second group.
- In a similar way, you can make groups of four by grouping together people who have cards of the same suit (hearts, diamonds, spades, clubs).

→

- You can also make groups of two or three, e.g. if you want groups of (three), select (three) cards with the same number. Do this for each group i.e. if you have 12 students, you'll need 4 x 3 cards. Shuffle the cards, deal them out and students form a group with others who have the same number on their card.

Use the cards for five-minute fillers
You can use the cards for short activities at the end of the lesson.
- Remove the picture cards. Write on the board: + = plus, – = minus, x = times .
  Deal out 2 cards to each student, e.g. 6 and 9. Individuals can make a sum with the two numbers, e.g. nine minus six is three; nine plus six is fifteen; six times nine is fifty-four.
- Remove the picture cards. Deal out a card to each student. Give everyone a task, based on the number on their card, e.g. *Number six? – Name six cities in Europe. Number ten? – Say ten words beginning with B. Number two? – Make two questions with 'Did ...?'*, etc.

Language and culture Step 1: Getting married
(coursebook p. 63)
10– mins
- To be used after the *Round up*, coursebook p. 49.
- You might like to show some photos of your wedding to the class, if appropriate.
- Allow time for students to read the text silently, then do the task.
- Encourage the students to do the Internet activity at home.

Downloads
- There's an activity for Unit 3 Step 1 which you can download from the Internet: www.langenscheidt.de/networknow/activities

Preparing Unit 3 Step 2

Intonation
5+ mins
- To be used after the dialogue, coursebook p. 52.
- After students have listened to the text twice, refer them to the *Lerntipp* on intonation at the end of the *Selfstudy* section on page 55. (Mention the section of Lerntipps on pages 190–191.)
- Have students repeat phrases from the dialogue, building up into repeating longer sentences.
- When you say the phrases, exaggerate the intonation *a little* and encourage students to copy it.
- Say: *Cover the dialogue. Listen and repeat:*
  1 *This is very nice ... (pause) – This is very nice wine ... (pause) – This is very nice wine, Anna ... (pause) – This is very nice wine, Anna – thanks. (pause)*
  2 *Tom did a cookery course ... (pause) – Tom did a cookery course when we were in Italy ... (pause) – Tom did a cookery course when we were in Italy three years ago. (pause)*
  3 *So, tell us about your visit ... (pause) – So, tell us about your visit to your grandmother's friend ... (pause) – So, tell us about your visit to your grandmother's friend in London. (pause)*
  4 *I came home early ... (pause) – I came home early because it was so cold ... (pause) – I came home early because it was so cold and wet. (pause)*

Scrambled weather report
2/11
5+ mins
- To be used any time after *Exercise 2d*, coursebook p. 53.
- **Photocopy *8 Scrambled weather report*** (p. 105) – one for each student.
- Cut the weather report into strips and mix them up.
- ↓ Play the weather report ▶ 2/11 again and let students work in pairs.
- Give out one set of strips to each student and ask them to rearrange them to produce the weather report from *Exercise 2d*. They should begin with *A It's ten past six and time now to ...*
- When students have finished, play the weather report ▶ 2/11 so they can check their answers. (Indicate the phrase 'a lovely day' at the left side which they get if they got it right.)

Language and culture Step 2: Gifts
(coursebook p. 63)
10– mins
- To be used after the *Round up*, coursebook p. 53.
- Allow time for students to read the text silently.
- Ask individuals to say *That's true* or *That isn't true* when you read out these 'facts':
  When you visit someone in England, ...
  – *you should arrive very early.* (Not true)
  – *you always take flowers.* (Not true)
  – *you give the flowers with the paper on.* (True)
  – *you shake hands with all the people there.* (Not true)
  – *you use most people's first name.* (True)
- Then students do the task and think of ideas for presents.
- If you have students from different countries in your class, ask them for a 'top tip' when you visit someone in their country.

Downloads

- There's an activity for Unit 3 Step 2 which you can download from the Internet: www.langenscheidt.de/networknow/activities

FYI Unit 3 Step 3

If you'd like to know more about the **history of Christmas cards**, go to www.langenscheidt.de/networknow/fyi.

Preparing Unit 3 Step 3

The first greeting card
2/16
10 mins

- To be used any time after *Exercise 4b*, coursebook p. 57.
- **Photocopy *9 The first greeting card*** (p. 106) – one for each student.
- In pairs, students read the instructions and, together, write in the missing words.
- Play the recording ▶ 2/16 again so students can check their answers.
  1 cards, 2 China, 3 greeting, 4 commercial, 5 post, 6 made, 7 popular, 8 money, 9 grandmother, 10 bought, 11 interesting, 12 museum, 13 married, 14 died

Language and culture Step 3: Invitations
(coursebook p. 63)
10– mins

- To be used at the end of the lesson.
- Allow time for students to read the text silently.
- Ask students about restaurants in the area which serve food from their countries.
- Write the list of types of restaurants on the board, and then add to it:
  Chinese, Indian, Vietnamese, Spanish, etc.

Reading: The tatoo
(coursebook p. 59)

- The Reading page can be done as selfstudy or read in class. You'll find ideas on how to exploit this in class on page 120.

Internet task

- To be set as an additional selfstudy exercise.
- Suggest to your class that they look at some e-cards cards. They should type 'Jacquie Lawson cards' into their search engine and look at the variety of cards.

Downloads

- There's an activity for Unit 3 Step 3 which you can download from the Internet: www.langenscheidt.de/networknow/activities

Preparing Unit 3 Now I can

Note: As the *Now I can* pages are revision and consolidation, you can use any of the optional and additional materials suggested for Steps 1–3.

Template 3: Get dressed!
15 mins

- To be used any time after the *Starter* exercise, coursebook p. 60.

Tip: Dice For this game, each pair of students needs a dice. Some teachers carry a set of dice in their 'teaching bag' because dice can be very useful in the classroom. If you don't have dice, students can make their own! They need one for each pair of students. Ask the class to find six-sided pencils or felt tip pens. With a board marker, draw dots, 1–6, on each of the six sides. Students can roll the pen in the same way they roll a dice.

- This game can be used to practise various structures, depending on what prompts you write in the dice boxes.
- This particular activity is to practise using the past simple, so write the following prompts on the lines in the dice boxes on the template p. 115:

⚀	⚁	⚂	⚃	⚄	⚅
– went	– didn't	– last week	– Why did you …?	– Were you …?	– two weeks ago
– saw	– wasn't	– when I was at school	– When did you …?	– Was …?	– last summer
– bought	– weren't	– yesterday	– Where did you …?	– Did …?	– I last …

→

- **Photocopy Template 3:** ***Get dressed!*** (p. 115) – so that you have one sheet of paper for each pair of students.
- Give out the papers and allow students time to read through the instructions.
- Put students into pairs and, if necessary, get them to make a dice (see the 'Tip' on page 87).
- Demonstrate the activity by throwing a dice and making a sentence with the phrase from the corresponding dice box.

Concerts
10 mins

- To be used after *Exercise 1d*, coursebook p. 61.
- Ask what sorts of concert you can go to (jazz, rock, classical, ...) and write the list on the board.
- Ask where you can go for a concert (concert hall, church, open-air, ...) and write the list on the board.
- Give the class five minutes to ask you about a concert you went to and to get as much information as they can – what sort of concert it was, where it was, when you went, who you went with, if you enjoyed it, etc. But you can only give short answers *(No, it wasn't. / Yes, I did. / ...)*

Downloads

- There's an activity for Unit 3 *Now I can* which you can download from the Internet: www.langenscheidt.de/networknow/activities

Getting ready for Unit 4

FYI Unit 4 Step 1

If you'd like to browse around a **gift shop in Canterbury**, go to www.langenscheidt.de/networknow/fyi.

Preparing Unit 4 Step 1

some / any
5+ mins

- To be used any time after *Exercise 3c*, coursebook p. 67.
- Prepare cards each with one of these words on: *the, an, a, some, any.*
- ↑ Make three sets of cards and have the class make three groups and do the activity.
- In class, shuffle the cards and invite a student to choose one and make a sentence with the word on the card.
- This student then takes the cards, shuffles them and invites another student to take a card, and so on.

A birthday present
15 mins

- To be used any time after *Exercise 3c*, coursebook p. 67.
- Get the class to stand up and make a chronological birthday line.
- Ask: *Whose birthday is in January?* When someone puts up their hand, ask: *When exactly?* Invite the student who has the first birthday in the year to stand at the front of the class and ask the other students to make a line behind him / her in order of their birthdays. Demonstrate that they must ask each other: *When is your birthday?*
- When the line is complete, check the order is correct by having students ask their neighbour: *When is your birthday?*
- Go along the line and pair off the students so they can work together.
- Say: *You want to give your partner a gift card* (Gutschein) *for a shop in your town or an online shop for his / her birthday. Talk together and find out your partner's hobbies and interests and then decide on a gift card for him / her.*
- Ask students to tell the class what gift card they decided to buy.
  Board: For *(name)*, I decided to buy a gift card for ... because he / she ...

Do you have ...?
10 mins

- To be used any time after *Exercise 3c*, coursebook p. 67.
- **Photocopy** ***10 Do you have any ...?*** (p. 106) and cut out the cards.
- Ask students to write a shopping list of three items from the gift board on page 66 in their coursebook.

- Hand out the cut out cards from page 106 so that each student has 2 or 3 cards.
- Explain that students have five minutes to find the items on their shopping list by walking around and asking other students: *Excuse me – do you have any ...?*
- If someone has the item on his / her card, he / she must say: *Yes, here you are* and give the card to the other student – even if it's a card with one of their items on it. If he / she doesn't have the card, the answer is: *No, I'm sorry, I don't.*
- Write the question and answer phrases on the board.
- When a student has found the three items on his / her shopping list, he / she can sit down.
- First demonstrate the activity by asking several students: *Do you have any (jam)?* And getting them to respond.

Language and culture Step 1: Cash machines
(coursebook p. 81)
10– mins

- To be used after the *Round up*, coursebook p. 67.
- Allow time for students to read the text silently.
- Ask the class to cover the text and write what they can remember about these numbers: Board:
  1967 £10 over 1 ½ million
- Then students do the task.
- Encourage them to do the Internet task at home.

Downloads

- There's an activity for Unit 4 Step 1 which you can download from the Internet: www.langenscheidt.de/networknow/activities

FYI Unit 4 Step 2

If you'd like to know more about the history of **Imperial weight** – and have a handy conversion table, go to www.langenscheidt.de/networknow/fyi.

Preparing Unit 4 Step 2

How much / many do you have at home?
10+ mins

- To be used any time after *Exercise 2a*, coursebook p. 71.
- Cut a piece of paper into 12 strips and give out one set to each pair of students.
- Students write an item of food or drink on each strip of paper.
- They exchange their strips of paper with another pair.
  NB: This is so they have practice with two sets of vocabulary – the words they wrote and the words they receive.
- Students put the strips face down on the table and, in turn pick up one strip and ask their partner a question with the word:
  How many (apples) do you have at home? – I have a lot. / I don't have many. / I don't have any.
  How much gin do you have at home? – I have a lot. / I don't have much. / I don't have any.
- Demonstrate the activity and write the questions and answers on the board as a pattern.

Shopping dialogue
10 mins

- To be used any time after *Exercise 3d*, coursebook p. 71.
- **Photocopy *11 Shopping dialogue*** (p. 107) – one for each student.
- Cut each dialogue into strips and mix up the strips.
- Give out one set of strips to each student (↓ or each pair of students) and ask them to rearrange the strips to produce a shopping dialogue.
- When students have finished, get them to read the dialogue with a partner.

Language and culture Step 2: Weights
(coursebook p. 81)
10– mins

- To be used after the *Round up*, coursebook p. 71.
- Write £ on the board and ask what the sign means. (pound)
- Write lb on the board and ask what it means. Students probably won't know so refer them to the *L&C* text on page 81 and ask them to find out.
- Allow time for students to read the text silently.
- Ask them to look in the text and find out how much one pound (lb) is (454 grams) before getting them to do the task.

Downloads

- There's an activity for Unit 4 Step 2 which you can download from the Internet: www.langenscheidt.de/networknow/activities

Preparing Unit 4 Step 3

Signs
10 mins

- To be used any time after *Exercise 2a*, coursebook p. 74.
- **Photocopy *12 Signs*** (p. 108) – one for each student.
- In pairs or in class, students say what the signs mean.
  1 You can get 20% discount. / You don't have to pay full price. 2 You can't shop here on Sundays. 3 You can go shopping from 8 o'clock to 9 o'clock. / You can't go shopping after 9 pm. 4 You have to pay here. 5 You can get money here. 6 You don't have to pay cash. You can use a credit card. 7 You don't have to pay. 8 You can't park here. 9 You can phone here.

Things to buy
5+ mins

- To be used any time after *Exercise 3a*, coursebook p. 75.
- Write six categories on the board and brainstorm vocabulary. Elicit four items for each.
  Board: drinks fruit vegetables milk products clothes cosmetics
- Have student make sentences with the items: *I bought a ... / I bought some ...*

Language and culture Step 3: Shopping online
(coursebook p. 81)
10– mins

- To be used at the end of the lesson.
- Allow time for students to read the text silently.
- Invite four volunteers to write the products from the four countries (England, Canada, America and Australia) on the board as they are called out.
- Encourage students to do the Internet task at home.

Reading: Markets around the world
(coursebook p. 77)

- The Reading page can be done as selfstudy or read in class. You'll find ideas on how to exploit this in class on page 120.

Downloads

- There's an activity for Unit 4 Step 3 which you can download from the Internet: www.langenscheidt.de/networknow/activities

Preparing Unit 4 Now I can

Note: As the *Now I can* pages are revision and consolidation, you can use any of the optional and additional materials suggested for Steps 1–3.

My weekly shopping
10 mins

- To be used after *Exercise 1b*, coursebook p. 78.
- Ask students to write a few sentences about their weekly shopping, using the ideas from *Exercise 1a* and *1b*.
- Then they swap their text with a partner, read their partner's text and find the differences: *I (use a credit card) but you (pay cash).*

Template 4: Flea market
15+ mins

- To be used any time after the *Exercise 1d*, coursebook p. 79.
- **Photocopy Template 4: Flea market** (p. 116) – one for each pair of students (there will be some pictures left over for next time).
- Cut out the boxes – each sheet of paper will give you twenty cards, each with a flea market item in it. Shuffle the cards.
- Divide the class into A and B. The A students want to sell things at a flea market; the B students want to buy things at a flea market.
- Ask the B students to stand up with a piece of paper and a pen.
- Give the A students 12 items each (deal them out randomly). Ask them to display the cards on their desks and decide how much they want for the items. When someone buys an item, they should be given the card – and the salesperson should keep a list of the items they sell and how much they cost.
- Tell the B students that they have 75 euros to spend at the flea market. They can look at the items displayed, ask how much they cost, and 'buy' items they like. They should write down each item and how much they paid for it.
- Demonstrate the activity by buying an item from an A student.
- After ten minutes, ask students to sit down and work out the total money A – they got, B – they spent, and report to the class.
  Board: Student A: I sold xxx and xxx and I got xxx euros altogether.
  Student B: I bought xxx and xxx and I spent xxx euros altogether.

Downloads

- There's an activity for Unit 4 *Now I can* which you can download from the Internet: www.langenscheidt.de/networknow/activities

Getting ready for Unit 5

FYI Unit 5 Step 1

If you'd like to read some amusing **Tube driver's announcements**, go to www.langenscheidt.de/networknow/fyi.

Preparing Unit 5 Step 1

2b A phone call (coursebook p. 87)

Tip: Pairwork (2) It's tempting for students to simply turn to the person on their right or on their left when they're asked to work with a partner. Try to encourage them to work with different partners. One method is to take lengths of wool or ribbon into the class (about 90 cm long and all the same colour) – you need one piece for each pair of students. Hold the bunch of ribbons in the middle. Tell the class that these are telephone cables and ask each student to take hold of the end of one cable. When everyone is holding an end of a ribbon, let go of the bunch. The students who are holding ends of the same ribbon work together in *Exercise 2b* and read the phone call dialogue.

Phone calls
10 mins

- To be used any time after *Exercise 2c*, coursebook p. 87.
- **Photocopy *13 Phone calls*** (p. 109) – one for each student.
- Ask students to work with a partner and hand out a sheet of paper to each student.
- Give them time to read the instructions and then they can act out the phone dialogues.
- Monitor the activity, remembering that the focus is on communication, so only intervene if communication breaks down.

Language and culture Step 1: The London underground
(coursebook p. 101)
10+ mins

- To be used after the *Round up*, coursebook p. 87.
- Ask what the underground is called in London (the Tube). Then do the task under the text.
- Give the class time to read the text silently.
- Ask students to write three questions about the text, beginning with *How many ...?*
- In small groups, students ask and answer the questions.
- Encourage students to do the Internet task at home.

Downloads

- There's an activity for Unit 5 Step 1 which you can download from the Internet: www.langenscheidt.de/networknow/activities

FYI Unit 5 Step 2

If you'd like to have a look round **Kew Gardens**, go to www.langenscheidt.de/networknow/fyi.

Preparing Unit 5 Step 2

Word map
10+ mins

- To be used any time after *Exercise 2d*, coursebook p. 91
- **Photocopy *14 Word map*** (p. 110) – one for each student.
- Give out the maps. Ask all students to write down a four- or five-letter word from Unit 5 Step 2.
- They are to give directions to their partner so he / she can pick up the letters and make the word.
- Demonstrate the activity: *You are at the bus stop. Go along this road. Take the first street on your left. Go straight on. Go past the letter P. Take the next letter. Go back to the bus stop.* **(T)**
  Now go along this road and take the first street on the right. Take that letter on the next corner. Go back to the bus stop. **(A)**
  Go along this road. Take the first street on the left, go straight on and cross the road, and take the letter on the corner. Go back to the bus stop. **(X)**
  Go along this road. Take the second street on the left. Cross two roads and take the letter on the next corner – the one opposite Q. **(I)**
  What's the word? **(Taxi)**

→

Records
10+ mins

- To be used any time after *Exercise 3*, coursebook p. 91.
- Board:
  He's / She's / It's one of the ______________ in the world.
- Say to the class: *Listen to this information. Write a sentence about each one.* Indicate the pattern on the board.
- Read out the texts, pausing after each one to give students time to write a sentence.
  1 *There's a hotel in Moscow – the Izmailovo Hotel – that has 7,500 rooms and suites plus lots of shops and restaurants. A double room there costs under 100 euros.* (biggest hotels)
  2 *Chihuahuas aren't big dogs, but Brandy is only 15 centimetres from her nose to the end of her tail. She lives in Florida and is often a guest on TV shows.* (smallest dogs)
  3 *Yao Defen is a Chinese woman who was born in 1972 and is 2.36 metres tall! She weighs 200 kilos and her shoe size is 57!* (tallest women)
  4 *The famous London department store, Harrods, had a pair of shoes for sale – for one million pounds! They were red and pink and had 642 rubies in them.* (most expensive shoes)
  5 *Every year, the American magazine 'People' makes a list of the world's sexy men! Winners include John F. Kennedy, Sean Connery, George Clooney and Brad Pitt. But what do you think? Who is your number one man or woman?* (sexiest men / women)
- Read the texts out once more.
- Check the answers in class and ask for any other information which they can remember.

Language and culture Step 2: Roads and streets
(coursebook p. 101)
10– mins

- To be used after the *Round up*, coursebook p. 91.
- Write Rd on the board and ask what it means.
- On the board write: 63 Albert ______________
- Ask if anyone knows another word you can have in an address – write their suggestions (in full, not the abbreviation) on the board.
- Refer students to the text *Roads and streets* on page 101 and allow time for them to read the text silently.
- In pairs, students do the writing activity.

Downloads

- There's an activity for Unit 5 Step 2 which you can download from the Internet: www.langenscheidt.de/networknow/activities

FYI Unit 5 Step 3

The pensioners travelled to Land's End, the most south-westerly point of Britain. It's the traditional start or end of journeys from one end of the country to the other – including the route of the Olympic torch in the 2012 London Olympics. If you'd like to find out more about **Land's End**, go to www.langenscheidt.de/networknow/fyi.

Preparing Unit 5 Step 3

Number quiz
10 mins

- To be used any time after *Exercise 3b*, coursebook p. 95.
- Read out the questions below and read out the two possible answers. Read each one out twice.
- Students write down the number they think is correct.
- To check their answers in class, volunteers answer the question with the number they think is correct.
  1 *When did President John F. Kennedy die? In* ***1963*** *or in 1961?*
  2 *What's the address of the White House? Fifteen hundred Pennsylvania Avenue or* ***sixteen hundred Pennsylvania Avenue****?*
  3 *How many states are there in the United States?* ***Fifty*** *or fifty-one?*
  4 *How many rooms are there in Buckingham Palace?* ***Seven hundred and seventy-five*** *or five hundred and fifty-seven?*
  5 *How many people live in Britain? About fifty million or* ***about sixty million****?*

The bus journey
10 mins

- To be used any time after *Exercise 3b*, coursebook p. 95.
- **Photocopy *15 The bus journey*** (p. 110) – one for each student.
- In pairs, students fill in the missing words.
  1 decided, 2 didn't, 3 used, 4 travelled, 5 England, 6 days, 7 travelled, 8 celebrated,
  9 seventy – **second, 10 birthday, 11 and, 12 friends, 13 day, 14 didn't, 15 sponsored**

The best and the worst
5+ mins

- To be used any time after *Exercise 4a*, coursebook p. 95.
- Board:
  I think ______________ is the best / worst ______________ that I know.
- Give prompts and invite individual students to make sentences with *the best / the worst that I know – footballer, city, car, actor, singer, Formula One driver, comedian, tennis player, TV programme, restaurant*

Language and culture Step 3: Double-decker buses
(coursebook p. 101)
10– mins

- To be used after the end of the lesson.
- Allow time for students to read the text silently.
- Say: *I went on a double-decker bus in (Munich). It was a sightseeing tour for tourists. And you?* Invite students to share their experiences.
- Encourage students to do the Internet task at home.

Reading: Taxi!
(coursebook p. 97)

- The Reading page can be done as selfstudy or read in class. You'll find ideas on how to exploit this in class on pages 120/121.

Downloads

- There's an activity for Unit 5 Step 3 which you can download from the Internet: www.langenscheidt.de/networknow/activities

Preparing Unit 5 Now I can

Note: As the *Now I can* pages are revision and consolidation, you can use any of the optional and additional materials suggested for Steps 1–3.

The map
10 mins

- To be used with *Exercise 2a*, coursebook p. 99.
- If you want to simplify – or speed up – *Exercise 2a*, make a copy of the map below – one for each student.
- Instead of drawing their own maps, students read Alun's mail and label the buildings.
  A: Chinese takeaway, B: cinema, C: Alun's house, D: bank, E: Italian restaurant, F: station

Read Alun's mail and write the names of the buildings.

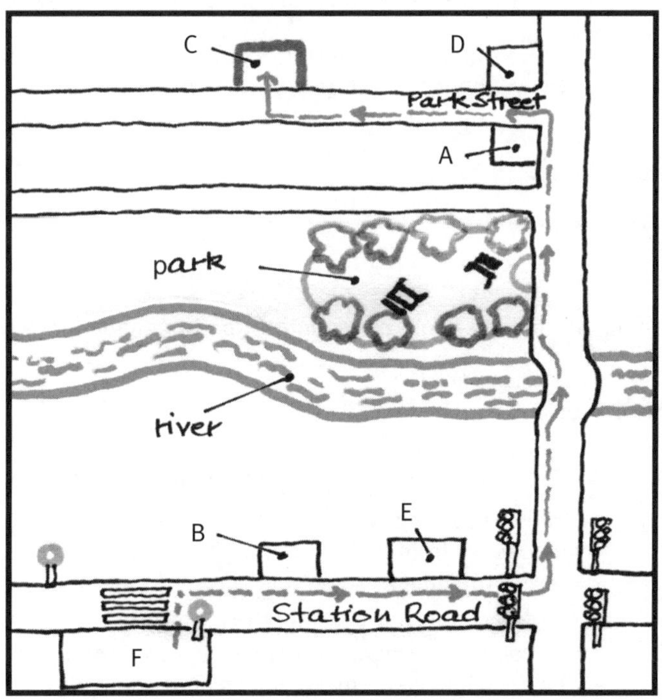

A: ______________ B: ______________
C: ______________ D: ______________
E: ______________ F: ______________

→

Dialogue responses
5 mins

- To be used with *Exercise 3*, coursebook p. 99.
- To simplify the task in *Exercise 3*, copy the list of responses – one for each student who would like one.

	Write the responses in the correct place in the telephone conversation on page 126.
A	Could you tell me the way from the station to your hotel, please?
B	Thank you.
C	Er, no, it's OK – but can I ask you a question?
D	Good morning. Is that the reception?
E	Bye.
F	Can I speak to (Petra), please?
G	Oh good, I can walk there. Thanks very much.

- In pairs, students first choose the correct response and then write it on the corresponding line on page 126 in their coursebook.
  D, F, C, B, A, G, E

Template 5: Telephoning
15+ mins

- To be used any time after *Exercise 3*, coursebook p. 99.
- **Photocopy Template 5: Telephoning** (p. 117) – one for each pair of students.
- Students choose two people on the page, talk about who these people are and decide why they're telephoning each other.
- They act out the phone call between the two people.
- Then, in class, they can each introduce their character and perform their phone call.
  Board: Photo (A) is a photo of me. My name is ... and I'm ...
- ↓ You can give topics for the phone calls, e.g.:
  A invites B to a party – what kind of party / when and where is it?
  A asks for directions to B's house from the nearest bus stop.
  A is ill and asks B to go shopping and dictates a shopping list.
  A wasn't at school last week and asks B to explain what they did in the lesson.
  A has a foreign visitor and asks B for ideas of things to do locally.

Downloads

- There's an activity for Unit 5 *Now I can* which you can download from the Internet: www.langenscheidt.de/networknow/activities

Getting ready for Unit 6

FYI Unit 6 Step 1

There's some disturbing information about **child emigration to Canada** on www.langenscheidt.de/networknow/fyi.

Preparing Unit 6 Step 1

Anna's email
5+ mins

- To be used after reading the email text, coursebook p. 104.

Tip: Repeat and complete After students have read a text, ask them to cover it. Read out sentences from the text but omit the last word(s). Students repeat the sentence and complete it with the final word(s).

Hi Dave. Can I ask you ...? (something)
As you know, I'm going to give my presentation on .... (Tuesday)
! If it's a long sentence, you can omit some phrases:
~~*First of all,*~~ *I'm going to start with some general information about my ....* (family)
! If it's a long sentence, you can break it up into parts:
Then I want to tell the class about ... (Faversham)
in the ... (1940s)
and show them some old ... (photographs)
etc.

Family matters
20 mins

- A development of *Round up 4b*, coursebook p. 105.
- **Photocopy *16 Family matters*** (p. 111) – one for each student.
- Tell the class that they are each going to give a mini-presentation of about two minutes. They should think of a good friend or a person in their family that they can tell the class about.
- Hand out a paper to each student and ask them to fill in information about their person and they can use these notes in their presentation. Reassure them that it isn't important to know *all* the facts about their person – and they can add other interesting facts about him / her.
- Allow about five minutes for them to do the writing, monitoring the activity and giving help where necessary.
- Ask individual students to present the person, using the notes they've made.

Language and culture Step 1: Emigration
(coursebook p. 119)
10+ mins

- To be used after the *Round up*, coursebook p. 105.
- Before the class turns to page 119, read out the first part of the text to them ('What do these Americans have in common:' + the list of names). Someone might guess their families were all from Germany originally – they were immigrants to America.
- Point out that *Emigration* = ‚Auswanderung', *Immigration* (the title of Step 2's L&C text) = ‚Einwanderung'.
- Give the class time to read the text silently.
- Ask what Germans introduced to America. (kindergartens; traditions, like the Christmas tree; food, like wiener, strudel, etc.; and language, e.g. 'Gesundheit!')
- In pairs, students do the surname task.

Downloads

- There's an activity for Unit 6 Step 1 which you can download from the Internet: www.langenscheidt.de/networknow/activities

FYI Unit 6 Step 2

You can read some accounts of **people who emigrated to Australia** at www.langenscheidt.de/networknow/fyi.

Preparing Unit 6 Step 2

Preposition game
10+ mins

- To be used any time after *Exercise 1b*, coursebook p. 108.
- Write the prepositions ON – IN – AT – FOR on separate pieces of paper and put one paper in each corner of the room.
- Ask students to choose a preposition and think of a sentence with that word. Then go and stand in that corner. Each student says his / her sentence.
- Say: *Change prepositions*. All students must go to another corner and say a sentence with that preposition. Continue for as long as time allows and interest is maintained.

Find someone who ...
15 mins

- To be used any time after *Exercise 2a*, coursebook p. 109.
- **Photocopy *17 Find someone who ...*** (p. 112) – one for each student.
- Give out the papers and allow students enough time to read the instructions before they walk round and ask their questions.
- If you have more time, ask students to make a horizontal row of four before they sit down.
- Everyone reports their (three) pieces of information to the class.

Language and culture Step 2: Immigration
(coursebook p. 119)
10+ mins

- To be used after the *Round up*, coursebook p. 109.

NB: This L&C is about Immigration *(Einwanderung)*; the L&C in Step 1 was about Emigration *(Auswanderung)*.

- Allow time for students to read the text silently.
- Students talk in groups and say which country they would like to emigrate to, and why.
- Encourage the class to do the Internet task at home.

Downloads

- There's an activity for Unit 6 Step 2 which you can download from the Internet: www.langenscheidt.de/networknow/activities

Preparing Unit 6 Step 3

Dominoes
10+ mins

- To be used any time during Step 3 as a revision of tenses.

Tip: Re-using materials Many of these photocopiable materials can be re-used. To save having to copy them each time you teach this lesson, print the activities on card, not paper – they'll last longer. You could even laminate them. If your copier has an enlarging function, you could double the size of the cards – then they are less likely to get lost. Count the cards in each set of cards before putting a rubber band round them and putting them in a clearly-labelled envelope:

NW Now A1 Unit 6 Step 3: Dominoes, tense review (Present simple, Past simple, *going to*)

It will take you a little longer the first time you do an activity, but, in the long run, it will save preparation time.

- **Photocopy *18 Dominoes*** (p. 112) – one for every three students. (Make a couple of extras in case some students play in pairs.) Cut them up to make a set of 16 dominoes.
- Students play in groups of three – or, depending on the number of students in the class, more able students could make a pair.
- Give out the sets of domino cards. Students deal them to their group (two students will get five dominoes and one student will get six) and the person with the extra domino puts one down on the table. The person with the end of that sentence or question places the next domino next to the first, reads out the sentence / question, and so on.
  ! Tell the class that punctuation is important – students should look out for question marks.
- Most people are familiar with the game dominoes, but you may have to demonstrate it.
- At the end, individual students read out the sentences.
  She visits her sister – every day. I saw my – neighbour yesterday. I'm going to talk – to her later. We had a – holiday last winter. I'm not German, – I'm Austrian. They aren't – going to have a big party. I don't often – clean the car. Does he like listening – to jazz? He doesn't want – to see that film. Did they look – for their tickets? Did you – phone her yesterday? We didn't say – goodbye to Anna. Is she interested – in history? He must be about – seventy. Are you – going to tell her soon? Do you – often watch TV?

Appointments
5+ mins

- To be used after *Exercise 1b*, coursebook p. 112.
- Not only photocopies can be re-used, you can recycle and adapt ideas, too. Look at the Tip 'Pairwork (2)' on page 91. This can be used to get students working with a new telephone partner and they should make an appointment without looking at the phrases in the book.

Language and culture Step 3: Dates
(coursebook p. 119)
10 mins

- To be used after the end of the lesson.
- Allow time for students to read the text silently.
- Ask a volunteer to come to the board and ask three students: *When is your birthday?* When students answer (e.g. It's on the twenty-seventh of August.), the volunteer writes it in numbers (the British way) on the board: 27.08. After three dates, ask for a new volunteer.

Reading: What am I going to do?
(coursebook p. 115)

- The Song can be done as selfstudy or read / listened to in class. You'll find ideas on how to exploit this in class on page 121.

Downloads

- There's an activity for Unit 6 Step 3 which you can download from the Internet: www.langenscheidt.de/networknow/activities

Preparing Unit 6 Now I can

Note: As the *Now I can* pages are revision and consolidation, you can use any of the optional and additional materials suggested for Steps 1–3.

Now me
10+ mins

- To be used at the end of *Now I can*.
- If this is your last course contact (i.e. if your course comes to an end before being able to use the *Globetrotter* pages on pages 121 and 122), get your class to think about how they can maintain their English (read and discuss the *Tip* on page 107) and what their plans are for continuing their English. Ask them to look at *My English* on the *Now me* page (page 120), write in the information and then discuss it with partner.

Optional & additional materials

Template 6: Conversation springboard
15 mins / open-ended

- To be used as a free-speaking activity at any stage of Unit 6.
- **Photocopy Template 6: Conversation springboard** (p. 118) – one for each pair of students. Cut the pages in half, vertically.
- Students work in pairs, A and B, and are given the corresponding paper.
- Ask students to read the instructions on their paper (and not to let their partner see!) and fill in the required information.
- They then tear off or fold over the instructions before swapping papers with their partner.
- In turn, students read out a name / number and first speculate who / what it could possibly be. After three guesses, they ask their partner why they wrote that name / number and ask questions about it to get more information.
- Demonstrate the activity by writing the name of the youngest person in your family on the board and inviting students first to have three guesses who it could be, then telling them and inviting questions about this person. Then write the year you came to this town and carry out the same procedure.

NB: This template can be used for a variety of prompts – simply write separate instructions, e.g. cities + objects, food + hobbies, buildings + clothes, etc.

Downloads

- There's an activity for Unit 6 *Now I can* which you can download from the Internet: www.langenscheidt.de/networknow/activities

Your notes

1 In my bag ... (Unit 1 Step 1)

- Work with a partner. Write the right words under the pictures. If you don't know a word, ask other pairs of students, or your teacher, *What's this in English? / What are these in English? Do you know?*

  book | brush | cigarettes | coins | comb | keys | letter | lipstick | magazine | mobile phone | newspaper | passport | pens | photo | sweets | ticket

- In turns, tell your partner what you have in your bag: *I have ... in my bag*. The first person to complete a row of four items (horizontal →, vertical ↓ or diagonal ↗↘) is the winner.

 ______	 ______	 ______	 ______
 ______	 ______	 ______	 ______
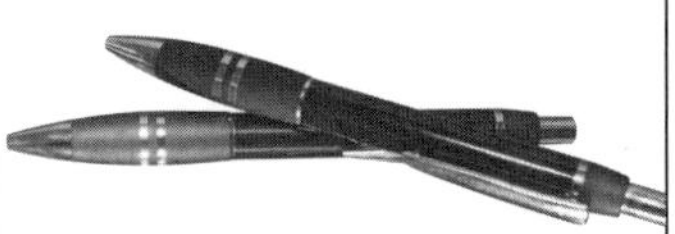 ______	 ______	 ______	 ______
 ______	 ______	 ______	 ______

2 Running dictation (Unit 1 Step 2)

Group A

Anna's from Canada, but her family was from England originally. Now Anna's in England for one year. She isn't on holiday. She has a job. She's a computer programmer. What are her hobbies? She likes history and she goes to a family history class.

Group B

Susan lives in Faversham. She works in a hotel in the town centre. She loves her job. Tom is Susan's husband. He was an engineer, but he's retired now. Tom and Susan are in the family history class, too. They met Anna there.

Group C

Do you know Dave? He's a teacher at the college. He teaches family history, but that isn't his job. He's the director of the museum. History is his job and his hobby. He has a lot of hobbies. He loves cooking Italian food and he likes classical music.

3 Famous people (Unit 1 Step 3)

Partner A

- Read your information about 'Mr Microsoft'.
- Ask your partner questions about Mr Bean so that you can fill in the form below.
- Then answer your partner's questions so he / she can fill in a form about 'Mr Microsoft'.

'Mr Microsoft'
William (Bill) Henry Gates

is an American businessman and philanthropist. He was born on October 28, 1955, in Seattle, America. He married Melinda French in 1994 and they have three children. His hobbies are reading, tennis and golf.

Mr Bean

Surname: ______________

Forename(s): ______________

Date of birth: ______________

Place of birth: ______________

Nationality: ______________

Occupation: ______________

Single ☐ **Married** ☐ **Divorced** ☐

Hobbies and interests: ______________

____

Partner B

- Read your information about Mr Bean.
- Answer your partner's questions so he / she – can fill in a form about Mr Bean.
- Then ask your partner questions about 'Mr Microsoft' so that you can fill in the form below.

Mr Bean
Rowan Sebastian Atkinson

is an English film star and comedian. He was born on January 6, 1955, in Consett, England. He married the Anglo-Indian Sunetra Sastry in 1990 and they have two children. And his other love is ... cars!

'Mr Microsoft'

Surname: ______________

Forename(s): ______________

Date of birth: ______________

Place of birth: ______________

Nationality: ______________

Occupation: ______________

Single ☐ **Married** ☐ **Divorced** ☐

Hobbies and interests: ______________

____

4 How often do they do that? (Unit 2 Step 1)

My best friend	Dave	**every week**	**always**
Anna	This class	**every day**	**usually**
My partner	The US president	**on Sundays**	**sometimes**
Our teacher	Susan	**once a week**	**often**
The German chancellor	*	**every summer**	**never**
*	*	**twice a month**	**at the weekend**

5 Questions (Unit 2 Step 2)

- Spielen Sie mit einem Partner / einer Partnerin.
- Verwenden Sie einen kleinen Gegenstand als Spielfigur (z. B. eine Münze, einen Anspitzer).
- Partner A startet mit seiner Spielfigur auf einem Feld in der obersten Reihe und stellt seinem Partner eine Frage mit dem Wort / den Wörtern auf diesem Feld.
- Partner B beantwortet die Frage, startet mit seiner Spielfigur auf einem Feld in der untersten Reihe und stellt seinem Partner eine Frage mit dem Wort / den Wörter auf diesem Feld.
- Ziel ist es, die Seiten zu wechseln. Gewonnen hat, wer zuerst auf dem Feld angekommen ist, auf dem sein Partner gestartet ist.
- Man kann in jede Richtung auf jedes angrenzende Feld gehen, sofern dies frei, also nicht von der Spielfigur des Partners besetzt ist.

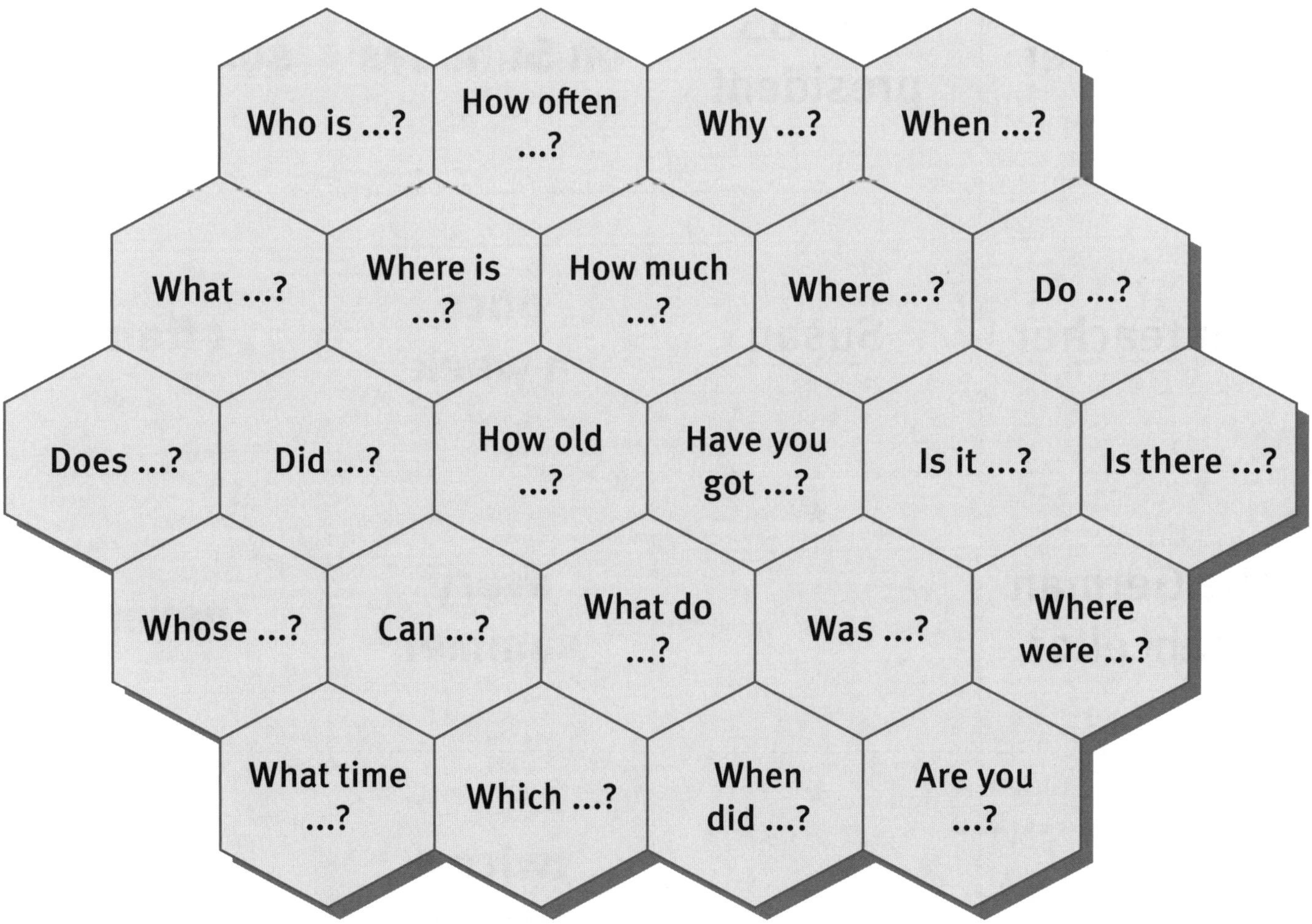

6 Crossword (Unit 2 Step 3)

Partner A

- Sie haben eine Hälfte eines Kreuzworträtsels, Ihr Partner / Ihre Partnerin hat die andere Hälfte. In Ihrer Hälfte sind die horizontalen Wörter *(across)* vorgegeben, in der Hälfte Ihres Partners / Ihrer Partnerin sind die vertikalen Wörter *(down)* vorgegeben.
- Stellen Sie Ihrem Partner / Ihrer Partnerin Fragen, z. B. *What's five down?*
- Ihr Partner / Ihre Partnerin gibt Ihnen Hinweise, damit Sie die vertikalen Wörter eintragen können.
- Beantworten Sie die Fragen Ihres Partners / Ihrer Partnerin mit Hinweisen zu den horizontalen Wörtern, z. B.: Partner B: *What's seven across?* – Partner A: *It's the capital of Ireland.*

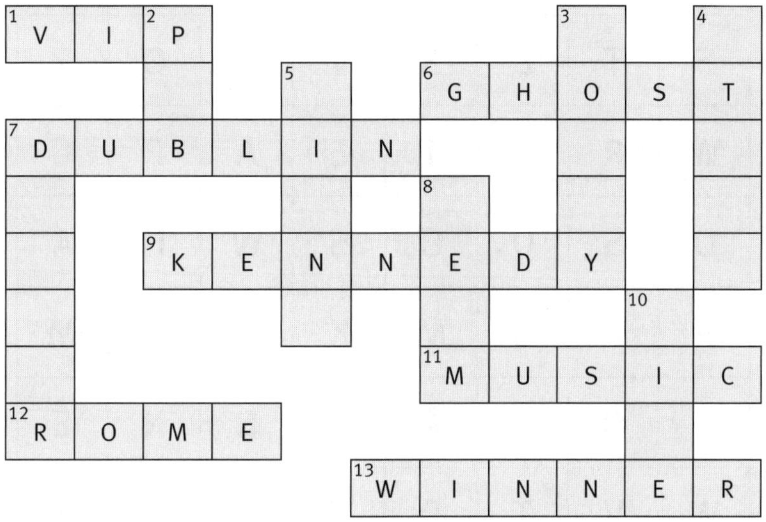

Partner B

- Sie haben eine Hälfte eines Kreuzworträtsels, Ihr Partner / Ihre Partnerin hat die andere Hälfte. In Ihrer Hälfte sind die vertikalen Wörter *(down)* vorgegeben, in der Hälfte Ihres Partners / Ihrer Partnerin sind die horizontalen Wörter *(across)* vorgegeben.
- Stellen Sie Ihrem Partner / Ihrer Partnerin Fragen, z. B. *What's seven across?*
- Ihr Partner / Ihre Partnerin gibt Ihnen Hinweise, damit Sie die horizontalen Wörter eintragen können.
- Beantworten Sie die Fragen Ihres Partners / Ihrer Partnerin mit Hinweisen zu den vertikalen Wörtern, z. B.: Partner A: *What's five down?* – Partner B: *She was the Princess of Wales.*

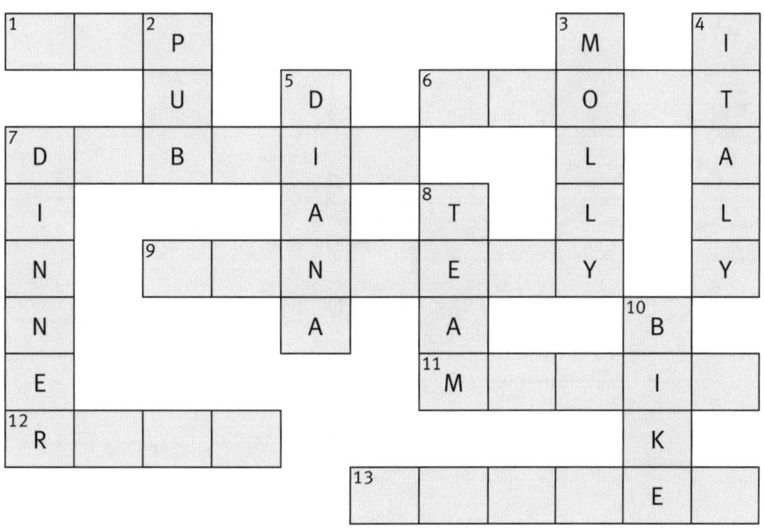

7 Wordsearch (Unit 3 Step 1)

- With a partner, find the past tense of 12 more verbs. The verbs can be horizontal →, vertical ↓ or diagonal ↘↗.
  Partnerarbeit:
  Finden Sie die *past simple*-Formen von 12 weiteren Verben. Die Verben stehen horizontal →, vertikal ↓ oder diagonal ↘↗.

S	T	B	S	V	S	Q	R
W	R	O	T	E	A	P	C
O	S	U	O	S	W	H	A
R	A	G	M	K	E	D	M
E	Q	H	A	O	N	N	E
W	V	T	D	V	T	E	T
E	E	R	E	O	E	R	W
M	B	L	G	L	C	O	I

- Write both forms of the verbs, e.g. *write – wrote.*
  Schreiben Sie die *past simple*-Form und den zugehörigen Infinitiv der 12 Verben auf die Linien, z. B. *write – wrote.*

1 ______ ______ 7 ______ ______

2 ______ ______ 8 ______ ______

3 ______ ______ 9 ______ ______

4 ______ ______ 10 ______ ______

5 ______ ______ 11 ______ ______

6 ______ ______ 12 ______ ______

8 Scrambled weather report (Unit 3 Step 2)

A	It's ten past six and time now to
L	look at the local weather. There are strong winds from the North
O	Sea today. People in Whitstable have a windy day in front
V	of them! If you want sunshine, Faversham is the place to be – with temperatures of around
E	23° Celsius. Lovely and sunny – perfect for gardening or having an afternoon walk. But no
L	afternoon walks in the Canterbury area – well, not without an umbrella! Rain, rain and
Y	more rain this afternoon and this evening. And a wet day
D	tomorrow, too! Pean Hill is a bit better – no rain but
A	a lot of cloud. So let's have some music to
Y	brighten our day – that old Simon and Garfunkel classic: *Cloudy* ...

9 The first greeting card (Unit 3 Step 3)

- You heard this story about greeting cards in *Exercise 4b*. Now read it and, with a partner, write in the missing words.
  Partnerarbeit:
  In *Exercise 4b* haben Sie die Geschichte der Grußkarten gehört.
  Lesen Sie sie nun und ergänzen Sie die fehlenden Wörter an den passenden Stellen im Text.

bought | cards | China | commercial | died | grandmother | greeting | interesting | made | married | money | museum | popular | post

Greeting (1) ____________________ go back to Ancient (2) ____________________ and Egypt. And in Europe there were (3) ____________________ cards in the 1400s. But the first mass produced, (4) ____________________ cards that you could send by (5) ____________________ were the idea of Sir Henry Cole. He (6) ____________________ the first commercial cards in 1843. And they were very (7) ____________________ – but they cost a lot of (8) ____________________. He sent a card to his (9) ____________________ and, do you know, in 2001, someone (10) ____________________ that card at an auction ... for £22,500! Sir Henry was an (11) ____________________ man. He was the director of a (12) ____________________. And later he started the National Archives where you can find out when people were born, when they got (13) ____________________, and when they (14) ____________________.
Yes, an interesting man.

✂- -

10 Do you have any ...? (Unit 4 Step 1)

cakes	cakes	cakes	jam	jam	jam
tea	tea	tea	coffee	coffee	coffee
biscuits	biscuits	biscuits	toys	toys	toys
games	games	games	glasses	glasses	glasses
vases	vases	vases	teapots	teapots	teapots
soap	soap	soap	tea	coffee	jam

11 Shopping dialogue (Unit 4 Step 2)

S:	Good morning. How can I help you?
C:	Hello. I'd like some cheese, please – not too strong.
S:	We have some very nice Cheddar. Or would you like this French blue cheese?
C:	The Cheddar looks nice. How much is it?
S:	It's £18 a kilo. This piece here is £7.20.
C:	Oh, I don't want so much. Could I have half of that?
S:	Yes, of course. And anything else?
C:	Oh yes – I need some eggs, too.
S:	These are nice and fresh. How many would you like?
C:	Er ... six, please.
S:	OK – they're £2.60 for six. Cheese, eggs – would you like anything else?
C:	No, that's all for today, thanks.
S:	OK – that's £6.20 altogether.
C:	Here you are. Thanks very much. Bye.

12 Signs (Unit 4 Step 3)

- Use *can / can't / have to / don't have to* to say what these signs mean.
  Verwenden Sie *can / can't / have to / don't have to* um zu sagen, was diese Schilder bedeuten.

13 Phone calls (Unit 5 Step 1)

- Work with a partner and act out these phone conversations.
  Führen Sie diese zwei Telefonate mit Ihrem Partner / Ihrer Partnerin.

Phone conversation 1

Student A	Student B
Phone your sister / brother (Student B). Say who it is on the phone. →	
	Greet your sister / brother (Student A).
← It's your mother's birthday on Sunday and you want ideas for a present. Ask for some ideas. →	
	Make suggestions for a present for your mother.
← Discuss the suggestions and choose a present. →	
	Offer to buy the present and take it to the birthday party on Sunday.
← Say thank you and then say goodbye.	

Phone conversation 2

Student B	Student A
Phone your sister / brother (Student A). Say who it is on the phone. →	
	Greet your sister / brother (Student B).
← Say you are ill and can't go to the party on Sunday so you can't take the present. →	
	Offer to take the present. Then offer to go shopping for your brother / sister.
← Say what you need from the supermarket. →	
	Make a shopping list.
← Say thank you and then say goodbye.	

14 Word map (Unit 5 Step 2)

- Work with a partner.
  Student A: You are at the bus stop.
  Student B: Think of a four- or five-letter word from Unit 5 Step 2. Tell your partner where to go to pick up the letters to spell your word.
  Student A: When you've collected the letters, tell your partner what the word is. Now it's your turn to give directions.

- Partnerarbeit:
  Partner A: Sie befinden sich an der Bushaltestelle.
  Partner B: Überlegen Sie sich ein Wort aus Unit 5 Step 2 mit vier oder fünf Buchstaben. Beschreiben Sie Ihrem Partner / Ihrer Partnerin den Weg, den er / sie gehen muss, um die Buchstaben Ihres Wortes zu sammeln.
  Partner A: Wenn Sie die Buchstaben gesammelt haben, sagen Sie wie das Wort heißt. Geben Sie dann eine Wegbeschreibung für Ihr Wort.

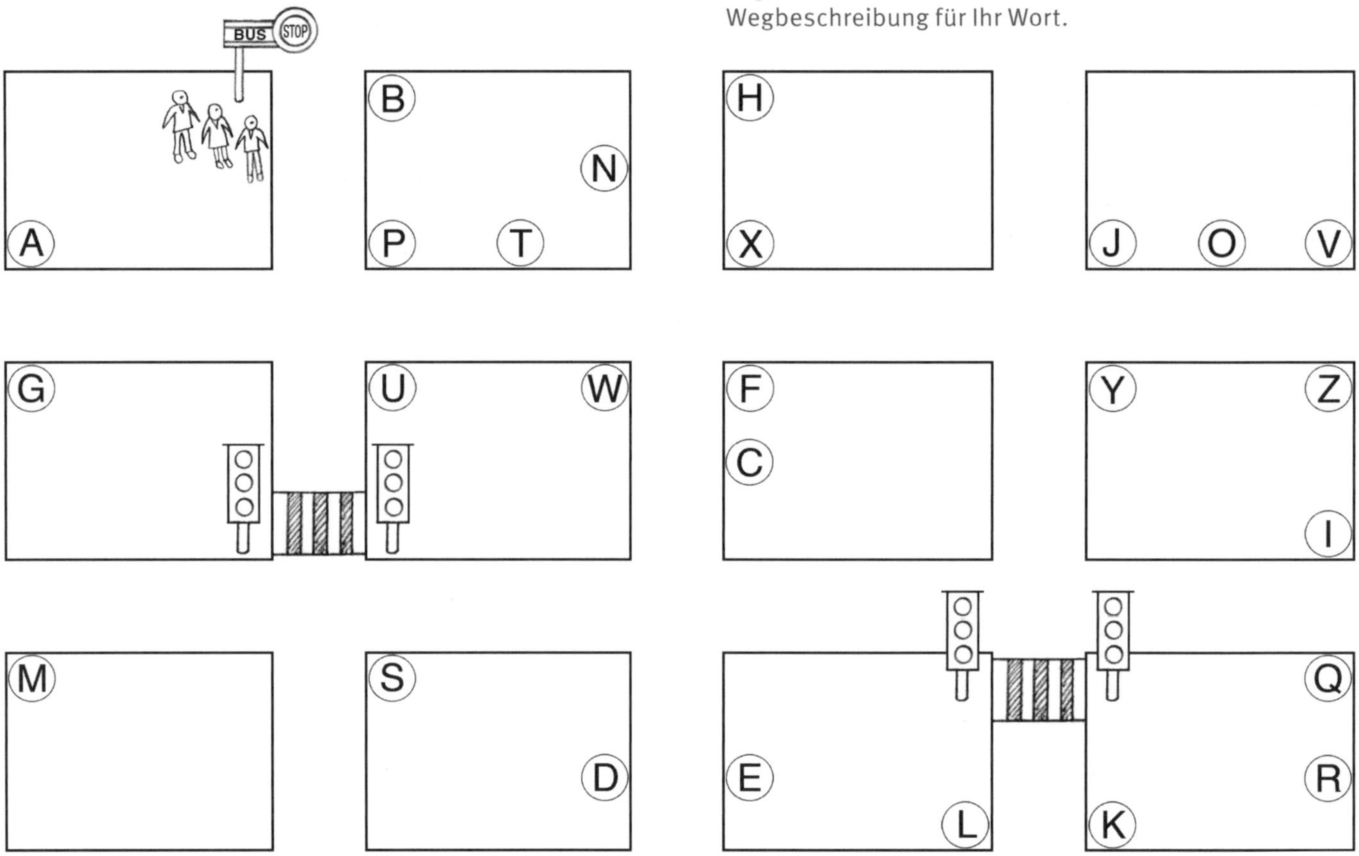

15 The bus journey (Unit 5 Step 3)

- With a partner, write in the missing words to complete the story about Sally and Fran's journey.
  Partnerarbeit: Vervollständigen Sie den Text über Sallys und Frans Reise.

Pensioners Sally Clarke and Fran Taylor (1) d _ _ _ _ d _ d to go on a long journey by bus. The journey (2) d _ d _ ' _ cost them anything because, in Britain, people over sixty can travel free on buses. The two women (3) _ _ _ _ d their bus passes and (4) _ _ _ _ _ _ _ _ _ _ d from the north of (5) _ _ _ _ _ _ _ _ d to Land's End in the south. They went on thirty-three different buses and were away from home for eight (6) d _ _ _ _. They (7) _ _ _ _ _ _ _ _ _ _ d eight hundred and eighty-eight kilometres and saw a lot of interesting places. Fran (8) _ _ _ _ _ _ _ _ _ _ _ d her (9) seventy- _ _ _ _ _ _ _ d (10) _ _ _ _ _ _ _ d _ _ _ while they were away (11) _ _ _ d lots of family and (12) _ _ _ _ _ _ _ d _ came to celebrate with her. But it wasn't all fun! One (13) d _ _ _, they got lost and they (14) d _ d _ ' _ have anywhere to stay. But they enjoyed their journey – and, because people (15) _ _ _ _ _ _ _ _ _ _ d their trip, they collected three thousand pounds for their local church.

16 Family matters (Unit 6 Step 1)

Name:

____

Relationship to you (aunt / grandfather / ...):

____

Born in (year and place):

____

Went to school:

____

Married? Children?:

____

Job:

____

Hobbies / likes / dislikes:

____

____

Extra information:

____

____

Why this person is / was special for you:

____

____

17 Find someone who ... (Unit 6 Step 2)

- Gehen Sie im Klassenzimmer umher und fragen Sie andere Kursteilnehmer/innen, was sie nach der Stunde vorhaben: *Are you going to ... after the lesson?*
- Wenn Sie eine positive Antwort *(Yes, I am.)* erhalten, schreiben Sie den Namen des Kursteilnehmers / der Kursteilnehmerin auf die entsprechende Linie.
- Setzen Sie sich, sobald Sie eine horizontale Reihe mit 3 Namen haben.
- Berichten Sie über die drei Kursteilnehmer/innen, sobald alle wieder sitzen: *(Stefan) is going to smoke a cigarette after the lesson. (Iris) ... (Klaus) ...*

Denken Sie daran, dass Sie immer eine Kurzantwort (*Yes, I am* oder *No, I'm not*) verwenden, und nicht nur mit *Yes* oder *No* antworten, wenn Sie selbst gefragt werden.

smoke a cigarette	listen to music	write emails	watch TV
phone a friend	have a beer	drink coffee	have a cup of tea

18 Dominoes (Unit 6 Step 3)

often watch TV?	She visits her sister	every day.	I saw my	neighbour yesterday.	I'm going to talk	to her later.	We had a
holiday last winter.	I'm not German,	I'm Austrian.	They aren't	going to have a big party.	I don't often	clean the car.	Does he like listening
to jazz?	He doesn't want	to see that film.	Did they look	for their tickets?	Did you	phone her yesterday?	We didn't say
goodbye to Anna.	Is she interested	in history?	He must be about	seventy.	Are you	going to tell her soon?	Do you

Template 1: A form

Family name: ____	Family name: ____
First name(s): ____	First name(s): ____
Place of birth: ____	Place of birth: ____
Date of birth: ____	Date of birth: ____
Nationality: ____	Nationality: ____
Address: ____ ____	Address: ____ ____
Tel. number: ____	Tel. number: ____
Mobile number: ____	Mobile number: ____
Email address: ____	Email address: ____
Job: ____	Job: ____
Free time: ____ ____ ____	Free time: ____ ____ ____
Family: ____ ____ ____	Family: ____ ____ ____
Likes and dislikes: ____ ____ ____	Likes and dislikes: ____ ____ ____
Languages: ____ ____	Languages: ____ ____

Template 2: Clocks

A

B

C

D

E

F

G

H

I

J

K

L

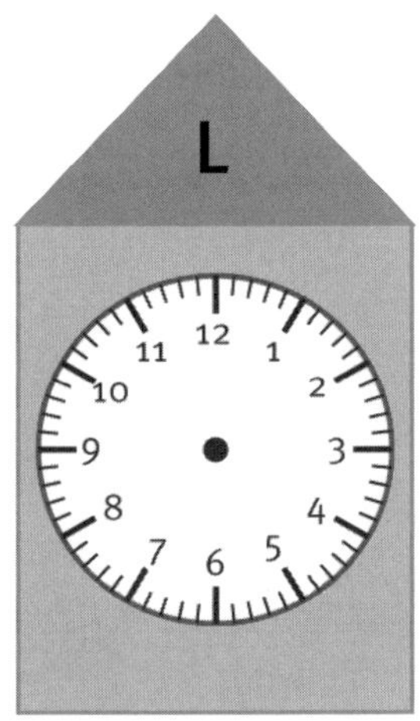

M

N

O

P

Template 3: Get dressed!

- Spielen Sie dieses Spiel mit Ihrem Partner / Ihrer Partnerin. Wer seine Figur zuerst komplett angezogen hat, hat gewonnen.
- Würfeln Sie und ‚gewinnen' Sie ein Kleidungsstück für Ihre Figur, indem Sie einen Satz mit einem der Wörter / Phrasen in dem Kästchen unten mit der entsprechenden Augenzahl bilden.
- Wenn Sie ein Kleidungsstück ‚gewonnen' haben, ‚ziehen' Sie es Ihrer Figur ‚an', indem Sie es an die Figur zeichnen.
- Wenn Sie eine Augenzahl würfeln und Ihre Figur das entsprechende Kleidungsstück bereits trägt, ist Ihr Partner / Ihre Partnerin mit Würfeln an der Reihe.

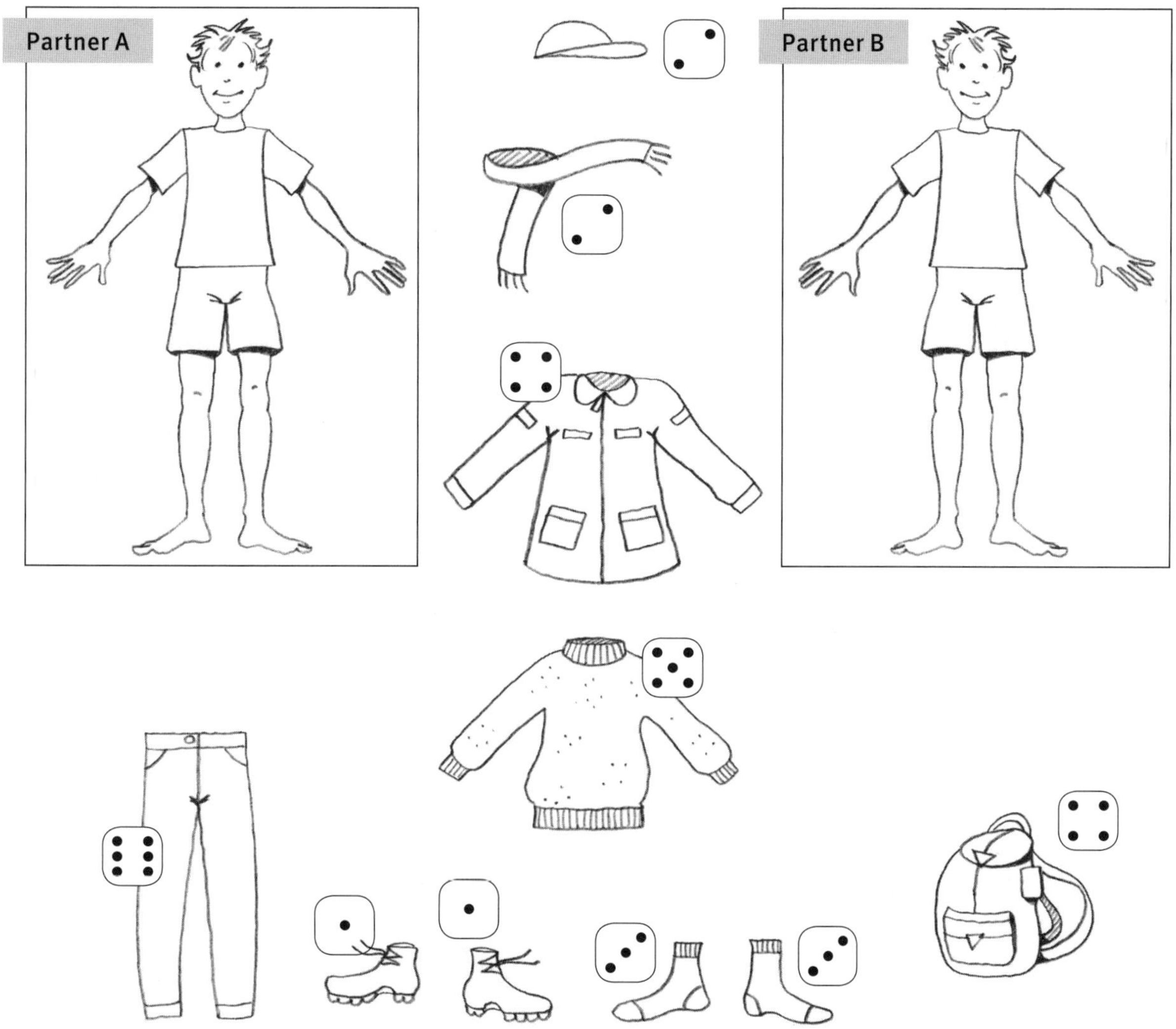

⚀	⚁	⚂	⚃	⚄	⚅

Template 4: Flea market

Template 5: Telephoning

A

B
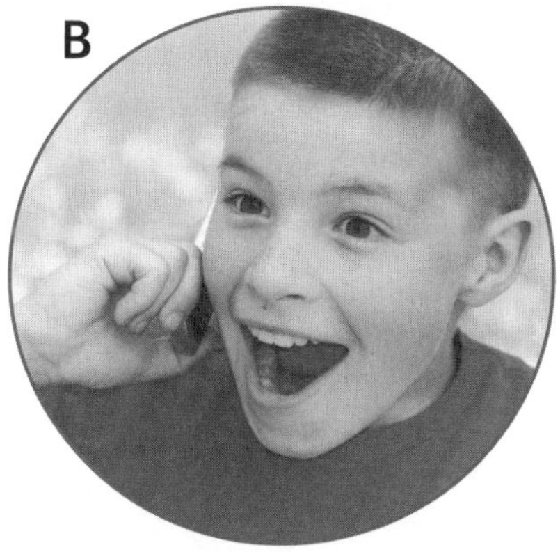
C

D

E

F

G

H

I

J

K

L

Template 6: Conversation springboard

STUDENT A

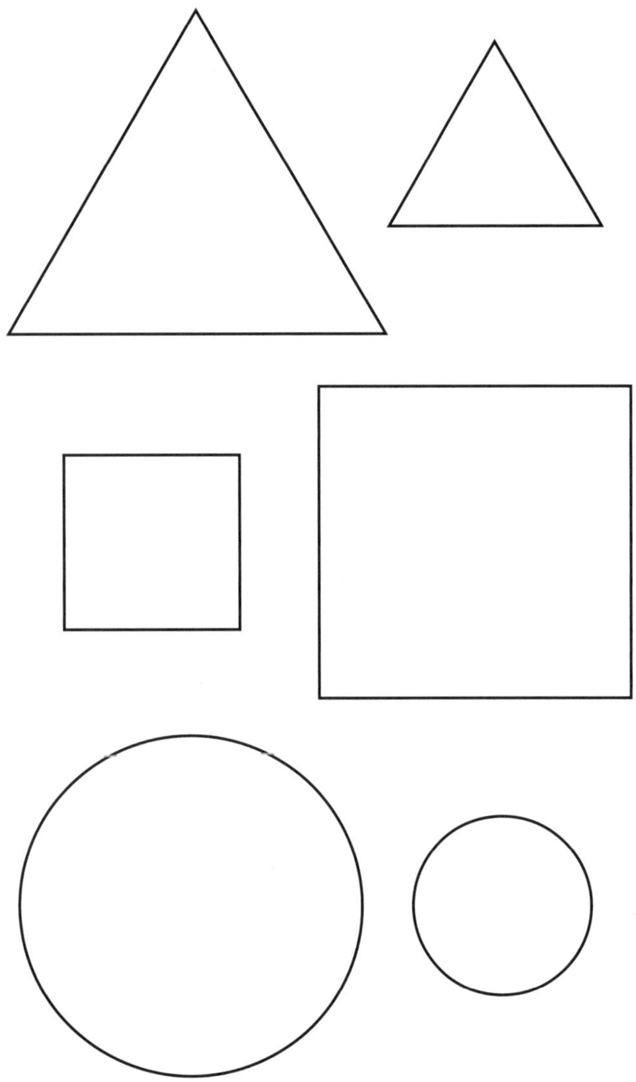

- In the big triangle (△), write the name of the oldest person in your family.
  In the small triangle, write the name of a teacher you didn't like at school.
- In the big square (□), write the name of one of your neighbours.
  In the small square, write the name of your best friend.
- In the big circle (○), write the name of someone you would like to meet.
  In the small circle, write the name of your best friend at school.

STUDENT B

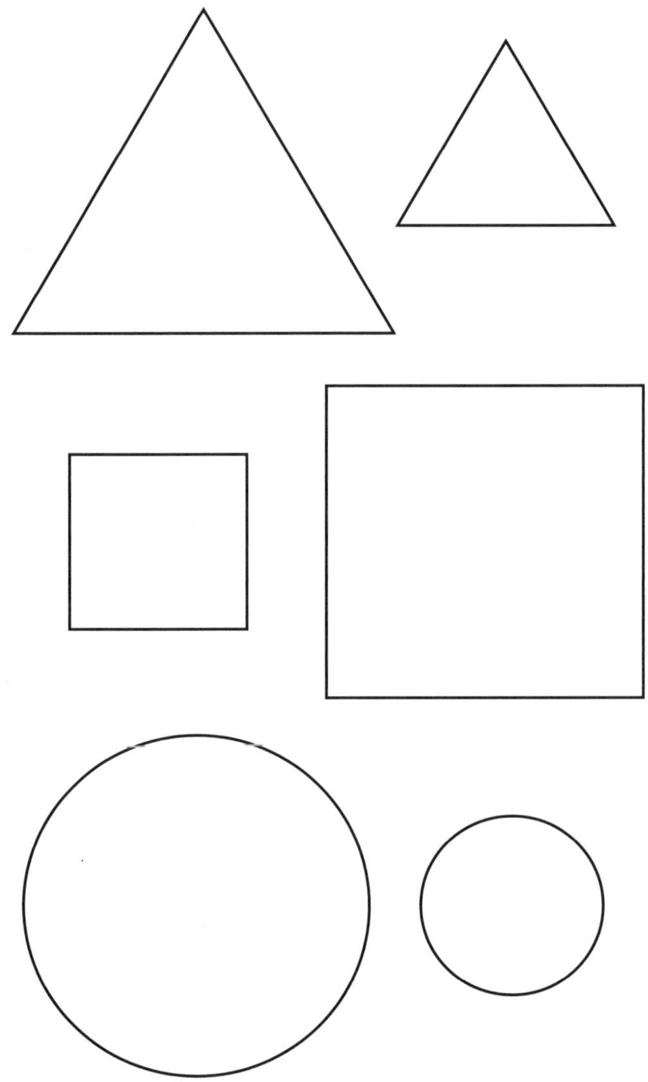

- In the big triangle (△), write the year you had your first English lesson.
  In the small triangle, write the number of people in your family.
- In the big square (□), write your birthday date – the day and the month.
  In the small square, write your phone number.
- In the big circle (○), write the number of plastic cards (credit cards, shop cards, etc.) you have with you.
  In the small circle, write the number of English lessons you missed during this course.

Ideas for dealing with the *Reading* pages at the end of Step 3

Throughout the coursebook, students are given dialogues and short texts to read and are presented with various tasks to practise different reading skills:

- **Skimming** – reading rapidly for the main points – for example, when you quickly read the front page of a newspaper to get the gist of what's in the news today
- **Scanning** – reading rapidly to find a specific piece of information – for example, when you read a train timetable in order to find the time of your train
- **Intensive reading** – reading a short text for detailed information – for example, when you read a contract
- **Extensive reading** – reading a longer text, often for pleasure, with emphasis on overall meaning – for example, when you read a novel

In the coursebook, the *Reading* texts in Step 3, the *Language and culture* texts and the *Reading* pages at the end of Step 3 provide the students with opportunity for reading longer texts. The *Reading* texts in Step 3 are part of the classroom lesson; the texts on the *Language and culture* pages, at the end of each unit, are designed for home or classroom use; and the *Reading* page at the end of Step 3 is part of the Selfstudy section of Step 3. But, if you have time, you might like to do one or two of the *Reading* pages in class, so here are some ideas on how to exploit the texts.

NB: The *Reading* texts contain new words so it isn't a good idea to have students read the texts aloud at first – unknown pronunciation will cause them to hesitate. A true reading task is to let students read the text silently and then do a task. If you want to extend the activities in class and get students to produce the vocabulary and structures, you can read out the text to them or play the CD.

Reading 1: At the Lost Property Office 1/24 (coursebook p. 21)

! After silent reading, comprehension questions, True / False questions or multiple choice sentences check that the meaning is clear.

- Refer students to the glossary at the end of the text. Students read the text silently and then choose the correct information.
  Board: The man wants to find his cat / dog. (dog)
  The man's name is Brown / Snuggles. (Brown)
- Play ▶ 1/24.
- In pairs, students write down the information for the form.
  Board: Owner's full name: ______ (Oliver Ian Charles Brown)
  Address: ______ (1 Manor Road)
  Name of lost pet: ______ (Snuggles)
- In pairs, students read out the dialogue.

Reading 2: Quiz time – riddles 1/51 (coursebook p. 39)

! Jigsaw reading or matching activities check that students understand the text.

- Before the lesson, photocopy this answer box so that you have one for each pair of students.

13 (T-H-E-P-O-S-T-O-F-F-I-C-E)	The letter E.
Smiles – there's a mile between the first and last letters.	Your age.
Four: **T**uesday, **T**hursday, **t**oday and **t**omorrow.	The letter T.
Twelve – the second of January, the second of February ...	In the dictionary.
A stamp.	Incorrectly.

- Cut out the cards so that you have one set for each pair of students.
- Refer students to the glossary at the end of the text. Students cover the second half of the text (the upside down answers) and silently read through the questions.
- Hand out the sets of answers. In pairs, students try to match the answers to the questions – they can ask other pairs if they need help.
- To check the answers, play ▶ 1/51.

Reading 3: The tattoo 2/19 (coursebook p. 59)

! You can use a reading text as a springboard for related activities.

- Refer students to the glossary at the end of the text. Students read the text silently and then answer the following questions:

Board:		
	What was the woman's tattoo?	(Her wedding present to her husband.)
	Why does she want to change the tattoo?	(Because the wedding is cancelled.)
	What is her idea for the new tattoo?	('I am lovely'.)

- Play ▶ 2/19.

Follow-up activities:
- Write the email the woman sent to the guests.
- In pairs, students act out the dialogue between the limousine chauffeur and the woman.
- Act out the dialogue between the woman and the tattooist the second time she goes to him.

Reading 4: Markets around the world 2/44 (coursebook p. 77)

! Getting students to retell what they have read to other students activates the vocabulary from the text.

Tell the class that they're going to read texts about markets. Ask about markets they know – maybe the *Viktualienmarkt* in Munich or a Turkish street market in Berlin or a local farmers' market. Ask what the markets sell and when they are open.

NB: You might prefer to photocopy page 77 beforehand and cut out the four texts so you can hand out the relevant texts to each group.
- Divide the class into four groups and allocate one of the four texts to each group. Give them time to read it and talk about it amongst themselves and ask you for any help with pronunciation that they might need.
- Then get the class to walk and talk ... they walk round and find someone from another group and they tell each other about the market they read about.
- After they have spoken to several people, ask them to sit down and listen to the texts while following in their books.
- Play ▶ 2/44.

Reading 5: Taxi! 3/19 (coursebook p. 97)

! To turn a reading text into a communicative activity, you can make an A/B missing information exercise out of it.

- Photocopy the following two texts so that each pair of students can be given Text A and Text B.

Text A

Patrick had (1) ______________________ in a small town. Patrick's Taxis was the only taxi firm in the town, so he had (2) ______________________. One day a second taxi firm opened in the same street, only a few minutes from Patrick's. This man put (3) ______________________ in his window: 'The best taxi firm in the town'.
Patrick was angry.
Then a third firm opened in the same street. This new man put a sign in (4) ______________________: 'The best taxi firm in the country'.
Patrick was angrier than before.
'(5) ______________________,' he thought. 'But what shall I write?'
Then he had (6) ______________________.
The next morning he put a sign in his window: 'The best taxi firm in the street'.

Text B

A German businessman flew to (1) ____________________ for a meeting. He took a taxi from the airport to the (2) ____________________. On the motorway, a BMW drove past the taxi. The man said to the driver. "Look, you see, it's a German car. It's faster than the other cars. Made in Germany – that's always best!"
A few minutes later, a Mercedes drove past them. Again, the German man said to the driver, "(3) ____________________. Made in Germany!"
Then an Audi went past. For the third time, the man said, "Audi! It's the fastest! Made in Germany!"
The taxi driver said (4) ____________________.
They arrived in (5) ____________________.
"That's £300 please," said the driver.
"What? It's so expensive!" protested the businessman.
"I'm sorry sir," answered the driver, "but it's my taxi meter. It's very fast. Maybe it was made in Germany."

- Students work in pairs.
- Hand out Text A to Partner A. Partner A reads the text in the box; Partner B reads the first text on page 97.
- Partner A then asks questions to Partner B and writes the missing information in his / her text.
- Follow the same procedure with Partner B and Text B.
- To check the answers, play ▶ 3/19.

Text A: (1) a taxi firm, (2) a lot of customers, (3) a sign, (4) his window, (5) I need a sign, too, (6) a good idea
Text B: (1) London, (2) city centre, (3) Another fast car, (4) nothing, (5) the city centre

Reading 6: What am I going to do? 3/40 (coursebook p. 115)

! A reading text can be exploited for vocabulary work – finding synonyms or rhyming words; you can also make gap-fill exercises with missing prepositions or missing verbs.

- Write the second and fourth verses on the board but leave out the verbs. Have students speculate what the verbs could be.

Board:

I'm going to ____________ a new start	(make)
I'm going to ____________ someone new	(find)
I'm going to ____________ a good time	(have)
And ____________ about you	(forget)
I'm going to ____________ you a letter	(send)
I'm going to ____________ you a song	(write)
I'm going to ____________ "I'm sorry	(say)
I'm sorry, I ____________ wrong."	(was)

- Play ▶ 3/40 so that they can check the answers.
- Students read the words of the song on page 115. Play the song in the background while they're doing this.
- Play the song once more and invite the class to join in the singing.

Your notes

Lesson notes for the optional *Globetrotter* (*Work* and *Travel*) pages

After Units 2, 4 and 6, there are two optional pages: *Globetrotter Work* and *Globetrotter Travel*. The three *Globetrotter Work* pages focus on work situations in a travel agency called 'Globetrotter Travel'. Here the students are presented with language and situations relevant to a working environment. The three *Globetrotter Travel* pages feature customers of the 'Globetrotter Travel' agency when they are on their travels, and present students with language and situations which they might meet when they're on holiday.
Each of these pages provides 45 minutes of classroom material, and a further 45 minutes of material can be found online. There's a code given under the title of each *Globetrotter*, e.g. www: A1GTAW (Coursebook A1, *Globetrotter A: Work*) which will take you directly to the activities online.

The *Globetrotter* pages allow for flexibility. Depending on the interests of your class, you may want to focus on just the *Work* page or just the *Travel* page; you could have a lesson consisting of both *Globetrotter* pages; or you may prefer to use just one of the *Globetrotter* pages and supplement the remaining 45 minutes with your own materials, or other optional materials from the previous units.

NB: It's a good idea to work out the number of lessons in your course to make sure that the basic 24 lessons (Units 1–6, Steps 1–3 + *Now I can*) can be covered before including the optional *Globetrotter* materials.

Globetrotter A: Work (coursebook p. 45)

Contents

Skills	Reading and writing emails
Vocabulary	American and British English; Computer terms

Lesson notes

Further classroom materials can be found online: www: A1GTAW

Starter: What's your job? 5 mins

- After students have prioritised the positive aspects of a job and compared their lists, ask for a show of hands for the most important aspect of a job.

Exercises 1a 1/58, **1b** 1/59 10 mins

- **1a** Read out the instructions and the list of jobs, then play ▶ 1/58.
  d) a travel agent

(M = Monique Sanders, I = interviewer)
I: Hello and welcome to 'Today in Town' on Radio Toronto. Today we're at the airport to talk to visitors to our city. Excuse me, do you have a few minutes to talk to us?
M: Yes, of course.
I: Can I ask your name – and why you're in Toronto today?
M: OK. Well, my name is Monique Sanders, I live in Ottawa and I'm here in Toronto today on business. I'm a travel agent and I have my own company, an agency called 'Globetrotter Travel'.
I: That sounds interesting ...
M: Yes, it is – I like my job very much. I'm very busy every day – I make travel arrangements, book flights or answer customers' questions – you know, tourists and people on business. People phone Globetrotter Travel to book vacations and we have a lot of business customers, too.
I: Do you travel a lot for work?
M: Oh yes, I go to vacation resorts to check everything is OK for our customers – and one day every month I visit our head office in Toronto.
I: That's a long way for a day trip!
M: Yes, it is! On those days I always get up very early to get the first flight. Sometimes I go home by train – it takes a lot longer but I can relax and work on the train. Today I'm in town to visit a customer.
I: OK! Thanks for your time, Monique, have a good day.
M: Good bye!

- **1b** Play ▶ 1/59 (Audio script: see *Exercise 1a*). Students ask and answer the questions in class.
  1 Monique lives in Ottawa. 2 It's called Globetrotter Travel. 3 She visits Toronto every month. 4 She usually travels by plane. 5 Because she can relax and work on the train.

Exercises 2a, 2b, 2c 20 mins

- **2a** Ask students to read the mail silently. Meanwhile write these questions on the board for students to answer in class:

– What sort of holiday are Peter and his wife interested in?	(an adventure holiday)
– Where do they want to go?	(Mexico)
– When do they want to visit the office?	(next week)

- **2b** In Canada you can hear some British English (BE) and some American English (AE).
  holiday: vacation, autumn: fall, car hire: car rental
- **2c** Students write the email and then exchange mails with a partner and read them.

Exercises 3a, 3b 10 mins
- **3a** 🔑 **1b), 2d), 3g), 4f), 5a), 6c), 7e)**
- **3b** Encourage the class to share Internet sites and links which maybe useful for their work, holidays or for learning English.

Globetrotter A: Travel (coursebook p. 46)

Contents

Skills	Booking a taxi; Checking in at the airport
Vocabulary	Contents of hand luggage; International cities

Lesson notes

Further classroom materials can be found online: www: A1GTAT

Starter: Departure 5 mins
- You can do this as a chain game: A: I always take my laptop. B: I always take my laptop and my phone. C: ...

Exercise 1 5 mins
🔑 **1 camera, 2 suncream, 3 plane tickets, 4 passports, 5 sunglasses, 6 phrasebook, 7 guide book**

Exercises 2a 1/60, **2b** 20– mins
- **2a** Play ▶ 1/60.
  🔑 **Address: 15 Bankdale Street, Collection time: 10.30 am, Arrival time: 11 am, Passengers: 2, Fare: $60**
  Play ▶ 1/60 again so that students can complete / check the information.

(T = taxi operator, P = Peter Carter)
T: Good morning, Green Line Taxi Cabs.
P: Hello, I'd like a cab to the airport tomorrow morning.
T: OK, and how many people is that for?
P: Two – my wife is travelling with me.
T: And what's the address, please?
P: 15 Bankdale Street, Russell.
T: Sorry, what was that address? Can you spell the street name, please?
P: Yes, it's 'Bankdale Street' – B – A – N – K – D – A – L – E.
T: Right, Bankdale Street, thank you. What time do you want the cab for?
P: 10:30, please. Our flight's at one o'clock.
T: OK, it's only half an hour to the airport. We can be there at 11. And which terminal is that?
P: Terminal 3.
T: Right, that's 10:30 am, to Terminal 3. Which airline is it?
P: Continental.
T: And what's your name, please?
P: Peter Carter.
T: Thank you, Mr Carter. The fare from Russell to the airport is $60.
P: Right. Thanks for the information.
T: You're welcome, sir. See you tomorrow, then, at 10.30. Goodbye.
P: Goodbye.

- **2b** In pairs, students roleplay booking a taxi.

Exercise 3 5+ mins
- Students identify the names of cities in English, and translate the names of some countries from German to English.
  🔑 **Bozen, Brüssel, Kalkutta, Kapstadt, Köln, Genf, Mexiko Stadt, Milano, München, Venedig, Wien, Warschau; Belgium, Germany, France, Greece, Italy, Austria, Switzerland, Spain, Turkey**

Exercises 4a 1/61, **4b** 10 mins
- **4a** Play ▶ 1/61 and students highlight the phrases they hear.
  🔑 **See audio script.**

(I = Ingrid Carter, P = Peter Carter, C = check-in attendant)
C: **Good Morning**. Can I see your tickets and passports, please?
I: Yes, of course. Here you are.
C: Can you put your **bags** here please?
P: **Sure.**
C: Thank you. The baggage allowance is **23** kilos. OK, your bags are fine. Now, do you have any hand luggage?
P: Yes, we have **two bags**.
C: Right. And where would you like to sit?
I: Can I have **an aisle seat**, please? And my husband can have the middle seat.
C: OK, just one moment, please ...
Here are your boarding cards. Mrs Carter you're in seat 17C, and Mr Carter in **17B**.
P: **Thank you.**
C: **Enjoy your flight!**

- **4b** In groups of three, students read out the dialogue, first using the highlighted phrases, then using the alternative phrases.

Globetrotter B: Work (coursebook p. 83)

Contents

Skills	Welcoming business guests; Making small talk; Getting down to business
Vocabulary	Conversation openers

Lesson notes

Further classroom materials can be found online: www: A1GTBW

Starter: It's good to talk 5 mins
- Students give their opinions on communication at work.

Exercises 1a 2/50, **1b, 1c** 15 mins
- **1a** Ask students to cover the text and play ▶ 2/50.
  Hassan (Allali), the owner of a hotel in Cairo.
  Play ▶ 2/50 again and let students follow the text.
- **1b** Students can refer to the text and tick the true sentences. When checking the answers, students read out the sentence from the text which gave them the information.
  ✓ 1 (Nice to see you again, Monique.), 3 (He's the owner of the Desert Sky Hotel in Cairo.), 4 (He's here for the Ottawa Travel Fair.);
  ✗ 2 (Nice to meet you.), 5 (Can I get you something to drink?)
- **1c 1c), 2a), 3e), 4b), 5d); Box A has the formal phrases.**

Exercises 2a, 2b, 2c 15 mins
- **2a Topics *not* suitable for small talk: money, politics, religion, your boss, your health**
- **2b 1 the visitor's journey to the company, 2 the weather, 3 sport, 4 holidays**
- **2c** Follow coursebook instructions.

Exercises 3a 2/51, **3b** 10 mins
- **3a** Play ▶ 2/51 and have students complete the phrases.
  1 would you like, 2 shall, 3 let's

(M = Monique Sanders, L = Liz, H = Hassan, D = Dave, P = Phil)

1 M: How was your journey to Canada, Hassan?
H: It was fine thanks – it's a long flight, but I flew business class – it was very comfortable.
L: So, you're in Ottawa for the Travel Fair.
H: That's right. I'm here for the whole week. It's always great to come to Canada – it's a beautiful country!
M: Thank you. Now ... would you like to sit down and you can tell us about package holidays in Egypt.
H: That's right ... My company has a new package deal for tourists from Europe and America ...

2 D: Did you see the football match on TV last night, Phil? Barcelona versus Arsenal?
P: Yes, I watched some of it in my hotel ... what was the score at the end?
D: Three – one to Barcelona.
P: Uh-uh – I don't really follow soccer in the States you know. It's not so popular.
D: Well, would you like to go to a game while you're here? The atmosphere at a live game is much better than watching it on television.
P: That's a great idea!
D: OK – let's do that. Now, shall we move over to the conference room?
P: Sure! ... Can I bring my coffee?

3 H: It's good that I have a warm coat with me – it's really cold today.
L: Yes, it *is* a bit cold. What's the weather like in Egypt at this time of year, Hassan?
H: Oh, the weather's lovely in winter – very mild temperatures.
M: Aah – very different from here! OK. So, let's get down to business.

- **3b** Follow coursebook instructions.

Globetrotter B: Travel (coursebook p. 84)

Contents

Skills	Checking into a hotel; Talking about past holidays
Vocabulary	Types of holiday

Lesson notes

Further classroom materials can be found online: www: A1GTBT

Starter: Good holidays 5 mins
- After students have prioritised what's important to them when choosing a holiday, ask for a show of hands for the most important thing.

Exercises 1a, 1b 15 mins
- **1a 1b), 2e), 3a), 4c), 5d)**
- **1b** Students write a definition of given types of holiday and read them to the class.

Exercises 2a 2/52–53, **2b** 10+ mins

- **2a** Play ▶ 2/52 and students identify the language the receptionist speaks and speculate on his nationality.
  He speaks Spanish. He could be Spanish / Colombian / Mexican / ...
  Play ▶ 2/53 and students complete the questions.
  1 Do you **speak English?** 2 Does it have **a sea view?** 3 Where's the **lift?** 4 What time does **the restaurant open?**

(P = Peter, I = Ingrid, R = receptionist)
R: ¡Hola! ¡Buenos Dias!
P: Oh ... sorry ... do you speak English?
R: Yes, of course, sir. Can I help you?
P: Yes, we have a reservation. Peter and Ingrid Carter.
R: Ah, yes, Mr and Mrs Carter. Welcome to Cancun. You're in Room 730 – on the seventh floor. You have a balcony and ...
I: Does it have a sea view?
R: Yes – there's a wonderful view from the seventh floor. Would you like some help with your bags?
P: No, that's OK, thanks. Er – where's the lift?
R: Over there, on your left, sir.
I: We'd like to have dinner in the hotel this evening – what time does the restaurant open?
R: It's open from 7 o'clock till midnight.
I: Excellent – thank you.
R: Thank *you*, Madam – enjoy your stay.

- **2b** Possible questions: **1 Do you have a hotel bar? 2 Does it have a balcony? 3 Where's the restaurant? 4 What time does the bar close?**

Exercises 3a, 3b, 3c 15 mins

- **3a** **1G, 2R, 3G, 4R, 5G, 6R, 7R**
- **3b** Follow coursebook instructions.
- **3c** First demonstrate the activity by telling the class about your best or worst holiday.

Globetrotter C: Work (coursebook p. 121)

Contents

Skills	Giving a presentation
Vocabulary	Words needed for business presentations

Lesson notes

Further classroom materials can be found online: www: A1GTCW

Starter: Hassan's presentation 5 mins

- Students suggest what could interest tourists about Egypt, e.g. the pyramids, Nile cruises, ancient culture, the desert, fantastic weather, ...

Exercises 1a 3/46, **1b** 3/47 15 mins

- **1a** Play ▶ 3/46.
  Start time: 11 o'clock, Room number: 127, Audience: About 100 people, Laptop? No

(R = Rosemary Brown, H = Hassan Allahi)
R: Good morning, Ottawa Travel Promotions. Can I help you?
H: Hello, could I speak to Rosemary Brown please?
R: Yes, hello, this is Rosemary Brown.
H: Hello, this is Hassan Allahi from the Desert Sky Hotel Group in Cairo. I'm going to give a presentation at the Ottawa Travel Fair next week, and I'd like to ask a few questions – you know, check on a few details.
R: Oh yes, Mr Allahi, the 'Tourism in Egypt' presentation. How can I help you?
H: Well, first of all can you confirm the time of the presentation?
R: Yes, one moment please ... OK, you're booked for 11 o'clock next Wednesday, 24th August.
H: 11 o'clock on the 24th. Right. And which room is that?
R: You're in Room 127 – that's on the ground floor.
H: OK ... Room 127. Thanks. And can you tell me how long I have – is half an hour OK?
R: Great. Thirty minutes is fine.
H: And who's going to be there?
R: Well, most of the people who come to the Travel Fair are travel agents and travel journalists.
H: And about how many? You see, I want to hand out some brochures so I need to know how many to bring.
R: Oh, I don't know *exactly* – but about a hundred.
H: A hundred?! That's excellent. OK, thanks. Oh yes – one more thing. I want to do a PowerPoint presentation. Do I need to bring my laptop?
R: Not really – the easiest thing is to put your presentation on a data stick – that's what most people do.
H: Right – that's no problem. I think that's everything. Thank you very much for your help.
R: Thank you for calling – see you next week. Goodbye.

- **1b** Play ▶ 3/47 (Audio script: see *Exercise 1a*) and students complete the email.
  The topic is: **Tourism in Egypt**. It's on **Wednesday**, August **24th**, at **11 o'clock** and it's in room **127.** ... – just about **half an hour.** Lots of travel agents and travel **journalists** come to the show every year, ...

→

Exercise 2 10 mins
🔑 **2 read, 3 beginning, 4 Speak, 5 language, 6 lot, 7 front, 8 correct, 9 questions, 10 short**

Exercise 3 15 mins
- Follow coursebook instructions.

Globetrotter C: Travel (coursebook p. 122)

Contents

Skills	Ordering in a restaurant; Asking about dishes on a menu
Vocabulary	food

Lesson notes

Further classroom materials can be found online: www: A1GTCT

Starter: Holiday food 5 mins
- Teach the phrase: *It depends* to help students talk about eating local food abroad.

Exercises 1a, 1b 3/48, **1c** 3/49 15 mins
- **1a** 🔑 **1e), 2b), 3c), 4d), 5a)**
- **1b** Play ▶ 3/48.
  🔑 **1 a menu in English, 2 a cocktail, 3 chocolate**

(P = Peter Carter, I = Ingrid Carter, W = waiter)
P: Excuse me!
W: Yes sir? Can I help you?
P: Yes, we'd like a table for two, please.
W: Of course. Please come this way.
W: Would you like a menu?
P: Do you have a menu in English?
W: Yes, of course. And what would you like to drink?
P: A beer for me, please.
I: And I'd like a cocktail – er, a margarita!
W: One beer, and one margarita. The special this evening is chilli con carne. We also have some excellent fish dishes. Let me bring you the menu ...
W: Here you are.
P: This menu's interesting – but a bit exotic. I think I'm just going to have the steak.
I: Oh Peter! You can have a steak at home.
W: Here are your drinks. Can I take your order now?
I: Excuse me, what's chicken mole?
W: Chicken mole? It's a speciality from Mexico. Chicken with chilli sauce.
I: Is the sauce very hot?
W: No, it's a mild sauce – and it has chocolate in it.
I: Chicken with chocolate!?
W: That's right. It's very good.
I: OK. I'd like the chicken mole, please.
P: And a steak for me – medium, please.
P: Well, that was a very good steak, just how I like it.
W: Can I get you anything else, sir? Would you like a coffee?
P: No thank you, not for me. Ingrid?
I: No, I'm fine, thanks.
P: Can I have the bill, please?
W: Of course. Was everything OK?
P: Yes, it was excellent, thanks.
W: Thank *you*, sir.

- **1c** Play ▶ 3/49 (Audio script: see *Exercise 1b*).
  🔑 **1 Excuse, 2 for me, 3 What's, 4 I'd like, 5 Can ... have**

Exercises 2a, 2b, 2c 20 mins
- **2a** 🔑 **1 dessert / Italy, 2 soup / Spain, 3 meat / Scotland, 4 garlic / Greece, 5 non-alcoholic / the USA**
- **2b** Follow coursebook instructions.
- **2c** Put the class into groups of three or four to role play the scene.

Exercise 3 5 mins
- Follow coursebook instructions.

Your notes

Christmas lesson – activities

FYI: Christmas is celebrated on December 25th in most English-speaking countries. Traditionally, on Christmas Eve (the 24th), before children go to bed, they put out mince pies for Father Christmas and a carrot for the reindeer that pull Father Christmas's sleigh. Father Christmas comes down the chimney at night and puts presents under the Christmas tree and in the socks (stockings) which the children have by their beds or which they have hung up on the mantelpiece. The 26th of December is called 'Boxing Day' because, in the past, employers used to give their house employees – the butler, the cook, the maids – their Christmas boxes full of presents on the 26th, the servants' free day.

If you'd like to do something a bit different in the lesson before Christmas, here are some ideas for activities. You can also find Christmas activities online in the *Network Teachers' Club* (www.langenscheidt.de/network/club – December 2009, Christmas activity file competition; November 2010, 'Network Now' lesson: Christmas activities (from A1 Starter or A1); November 2011, Christmas).

Activities from Section 1 can be used after completing Unit 2.
Activities from Section 1 + 2 can be used after completing Unit 4.
Activities from Sections 1, 2 + 3 can be used after completing Unit 6.

Section 1:

Activity 1a: Christmas presents

- Write the words CHRISTMAS PRESENTS on the board, vertically.
- Students call out as many presents as they can think of for each letter of the two words. e.g. **Cat, Holiday, Rum, Italian meal, Scrabble, Tea, Make-up, Alcohol, Skis,** etc.

Activity 1b: Pass the parcel

- This activity requires quite a bit of preparation. You will need a small present, wrapping paper (you could use coloured pages of a magazine or serviettes) and sticky tape.
- **Copy Activity 1b** (p. 128) and cut out the cards (or you could write the phrases on post-its). Wrap the present and stick a phrase on the wrapping paper. Continue doing this so that there's a phrase on each layer of wrapping paper.
- Show the class the parcel and explain they can unwrap it – but first they must make a sentence with the phrase. Read the phrase on the outer layer. Students volunteer to make a sentence. The person holding the parcel chooses someone to make a sentence. The person who makes a correct sentence can take off one layer of paper and read out the next phrase to the class. Continue until the last layer is reached and the present is revealed.

Section 2:

Activity 2a: In my country / family ...

- **Copy Activity 2a** (p. 128) – one for each pair of students. Cut out the cards, keeping the adverbs and the time phrases in separate piles.
- Students put the two piles of cards face-down on the desk.
- Remind students what the Christmas days are called in English.

  Board:
  Christmas Eve: December 24th
  Christmas Day: December 25th
  Boxing Day: December 26th
  New Year's Eve: December 31st
  New Year's Day: January 1st
- Demonstrate the activity with an able student. Pick up a card from each pile and ask a question with the phrases, e.g. *What do you (usually) do on (Christmas Day)?*
- In pairs, students ask and answer the questions.

Activity 2b: Jingle Bells

NB: The song was written by the American James Pierpoint in the 1850s. And it was the first song to be broadcast from Space! In December, 1965, the astronauts on Gemini 6 played the *Jingle Bells* on a mouth organ they had smuggled on board and the crew sang *Jingle Bells*.

- **Copy Activity 2b** (see last page of the TRB) – one for each student.
- Read out the text and have students repeat.
- If you have a recording of the song, play it to the class, inviting them to join in. Otherwise, you can lead the singing (that isn't too daunting as the melody of *Jingle Bells* will be familiar to them!) – and ask them to have their house keys or car keys ready to jingle when they sing the phrase *Jingle Bells*.

Christmas lesson

Section 3:
Activity 3a:
Christmas Day

- Tell the class about your plans for Christmas Day, e.g. *This year I'm going to have a perfect Christmas. I'm going to sleep till ten o'clock and then I'm going to have breakfast in bed. I'm going to get up and have a shower and then I'm going to start cooking the turkey. I'm going to phone my mother and say Happy Christmas. My husband and I are going to have a traditional Christmas dinner at about 7 pm. And then we're going to open our presents. Later, we're going to watch a nice DVD. We aren't going to have any stress!*
- Invite students to ask you questions about your Christmas.
- Ask students to think about their next Christmas Day and make a few notes about it.
- In small groups, students talk about their next Christmas Day and ask and answer questions about it.

Activity 3b:
How many people ...?

- **Copy Activity 3b** (see last page of the TRB) – one for each student.
- Board: All of us ...
  Most of us ...
  Some of us ...
  (Three) of us ...
  None of us ...
- Demonstrate the activity by asking each student: *Do you eat fish at Christmas?* Present your conclusion by completing the appropriate sentence on the board.
- Make groups of four or five and hand out the papers. Students work together in their group and complete the questionnaire.
- Ask a spokesman for each group to report their findings.

Christmas lesson – photocopiable materials

Activity 1b: Pass the parcel

Christmas Eve	Boxing Day	Christmas tree	Christmas cards	December 24th	Silent Night
Christmas shopping	presents	turkey	Father Christmas	television	church

Activity 2a: In my country / family ...

always	on New Year's Eve
usually	on Christmas Day
often	on Boxing Day
sometimes	on New Year's Eve
never	on New Year's Day